THE SECRET BOOK
OF RUNNING

///

Lance P. Martin

For the Trauma Whisperer, VO2Max,

and Captain LE/O

///

Table of Contents

Introduction—Speaking Truth to PR

Runner, this book is for you. Unless you're an elite runner or that pernicious subset, the local elite runner, in which case you don't need to learn any secrets and this book is not for you. But if you are an elite runner and you're buying it as a gift, then get a copy by all means, but otherwise put it down, go have a protein shake, Nair your legs, and leave it for the people who need it. Please don't read it. For if you are in the top 1% in all your races, this book is probably not for you and it is simply not fair for you to gain another advantage. And at the other extreme, if you're one step ahead of the street sweeper, if you don't run a single step at your races, if you have a hard time distinguishing between a race and a parade, if your race gear has ever included a parasol, if you've ever texted while on the course, this book is probably not for you either. Not to diminish your accomplishments—far from it. It's just that this is the secret book of running, not the secret book of walking, second-lining, loitering, or any other comparable form of movement on a city or county road.

For everyone else, this book is for you. This book is for the average runner, the person in the pack, whether you are a front packer, a mid-packer, a backpacker, or a Green Bay Packer. If you are on the road or the treadmill, or both— but not at the same time—three to seven days a week, this book is for you. But wait, you say, I only run two days per week. Can I still get the book? Well, as much as we want to sell copies and spread these secrets, we would like to see, at a minimum, three days of running per week. True runners can be a sensitive band, and if we let you read the book, they might consider their tribe cheapened. And yet we hate to deny you the secret advice contained in this book, for who knows, it just might inspire you to go beyond two days, to increase your effort, to build to committed training regimen and perhaps one day become a Beatles runner—eight days a week. So go ahead, you two-timers, get the book, but let's hold off on the title "runner" for now. Let's make that title a goal to aspire towards.

How about me, I run just once a week? Can I read the book? Sorry, pal, we have to draw the line somewhere.

Now that we have our special, select audience, our as-signed corral of readers, let's talk about this wonderful, mys-terious, painful, uplifting, frustrating, and addictive thing we call running. Do you remember why you started running? Was it to improve your health? Was it to raise money for charity? Was it because you lost a bet? Was it out of a sense of civic obligation to train for your town's official race? Was it a quest for the fabled "runner's high"? (If it was the last one and it's a high you're after, have you learned that it would have been easier to ask the kid who mows your lawn to tell you where he gets his stash?)

Whether you started running last month, last year, or last decade, you had a reason for doing so. And while you may not remember why you started running, if you're still running you know why you run now. The ancient Greeks had a phrase for it: That Runner. You know the one we mean. You don't have to say That Runner's name out loud, but it's fine to picture him or her in your mind's eye and clench your jaw. Not too tight, unless you have a Cadillac dental plan at work. That Runner. You could say that it is the cornerstone of the secret training advice imparted in these pages. That Runner. Flare your nostrils if you must. Maybe he's your training partner. Maybe she's the perky one at the races. What is certain is that he or she is finishing ahead of you. That Runner is faster that you, and it's eating at you like rust in Detroit. That Runner sashays into your thoughts during training and at races. You loathe the way that bobbing ponytail mocks you 5K after 5K, especially if it's one of those graying, sensitive-dude ponytails.

But does it drive you to get up and out the door every morning, regardless of the weather, unless it's too cold or hot or dark or hazy or you're tired or would rather have coffee and a Pop-Tart? When you finish this book, it will. Let's face it: That Runner is just about ruining this sport for you. At this point you may say, I once heard that the beauty of running is that the only person you're competing against is yourself. You know who came up with that bit of wisdom? That Runner!

Having examined countless test subjects over the years, we have discovered that there are only two types of runners really. One type is the runner who has that person in mind that he must beat even if it becomes such an all-consuming obsession that he ends up becoming the very thing he sought to defeat—think Anakin and Obi-Wan with timing chips instead of light sabers. The other type is the runner who has yet to admit this fact. And if you don't think you fit into either of these categories, here is our response:

Welcome to the wonderful world of running. This must be your first day.

Rest assured that this book is the answer to your prayers, even though, with all the problems in the world, you ought to be praying for an end to genocide or oil spills, not to beat That Runner in a local race or that some calamity, be it turf toe or a chronic addiction to bear claws, befall him or her. After you read this book, you will know how to put That Runner in your rearview mirror for good. We will share with you all the secret tips and tricks you will need to noogie That Runner into submission. (We are speaking metaphorically, of course, unless you race him or her in the Noogie Boogie, the infamous 10K where on-course noogies are permitted.)

At this point, you may be asking yourself: If I truly want to improve my running, why shouldn't I go the bookstore or my local running store and buy one of the classic treatises on running? Or why not subscribe to a glossy running magazine? They are, after all, filled with seductive, color-coded training plans. With the highest sense of objectivity that we can summon, we say don't bother. First of all, those books are too long. The Lore of Running may be the Bible, Constitution, and Harry Potter series all rolled into one, but if you take the time to read it, you'll never have time to train. Besides, the training programs you will find in books and magazines are not for you. Do you really want a twenty-four-week program with macro-cycles, mini-cycles, uni-cycles, and tri-cycles? No. Unless you're a Shriner at a parade or you're doing Motocross, you don't need a mini-cycle.

How about the Internet, you say? It has a trove of running advice. Again, all that information is wrong for you, if not plain wrong. To paraphrase Mark Twain, there are three types of lies: lies, damn lies, and running advice. If you spend a little time on the Internet, it won't take long for you to read one of the greatest lies ever foisted on runners: Listen to your body. What a side-splitter! For those who say we should listen to our body, we respond: Which part? Because when we listen to our legs, they say: Go back to bed. We're asleep. That's why we're tingly. And when we listen to our stomach, it says: Dunkin! Dunkin! And when we listen to our head, it says: If you get into work early and return that petty cash, no one will ever know. Unless a training plan instructs you to ignore your body, no matter how much it pleads with or screams at you, it is a fraudulent plan foisted on an un-suspecting public by what we can only describe as a Secret Cabal of Coaches and Trainers, or SCOCATs for short.

You need this book because it will dispel all the false running myths currently in print. It will reveal the truth to you. It will not offer you any "latest advances" in the science of running. There will be no double blind clinical trials. This book contains the information that the running establish-ment doesn't want you to know. We will guide you through the published methods and theories of the SCOCATs, "Da Vinci Code" style, and expose their secrets and lies. We will share the information they don't want you to know about and debunk the misinformation they spread in books and magazines to confuse you and keep you slower than That Runner.

You need to understand that the SCOCATs date back to the founding of the Republic. Thy have been gathering and conspiring under a veil of secrecy at least as long as the Freemasons, Skull and Bones, the Trilateral Commission, and many of the other strange groups you may remember from watching *The X-Files*. They have been behind every significant running and racing decision in the last two hundred years. Did you ever wonder why men's running shorts are so short? It was part of an early initiation ritual meant to humiliate men, but someone leaked the design to a shirtwaist manufacturer in Philadelphia and the rest is history. Did you ever wonder why all our races are measured in kilometers, even though America long ago gave a collective middle finger (two-liter Cokes excepted) to the metric system? The early SCOCATs were rabid Europhiles. Did you ever stare at that Unicorn logo on the back of those Boston Marathon windbreakers—you know, the one that every Boston marathon runner comes back with and wears to every gathering where you are present, including court appearances, church services, and the birth of a child? (What do they do, give them out at the finish line and exhort these naturally gifted runners to go forth and gloat?) That unicorn is an ancient SCOCAT cult symbol, just as surely as the eye in the pyramid on the back of a dollar bill, and Mickey Mouse.

So the first thing we will do is arm you with the truth about how to train properly. We will walk you through the real biological processes at work in training and racing and the true conclusions about exercise physiology. Once you have these background principles firmly in hand, we will teach you the JAR Method of training. The JAR method channels your Jealousy, Anger, and Resentment as to That Runner so you can train and race at a level you never imagined. If your body is a bumper car, JAR is the electrified antenna that powers it so you can kamikaze full-speed into the back of That Runner. Once you learn the JAR Method, we will show you how to implement it at every race distance and in every race condition.

We hope this introductory appetizer is enough to keep your reading the book. If it is not, then That Runner thanks you for not turning the page. But if it is, then read on runner and gobble up the secrets we have to impart the way you soon will be gobbling up negative splits, extra miles, and That Runner.

A Brief History of Running

Before we reveal the secrets of running, we should spend a moment appreciating running's rich history, for you shall soon hold a hallowed place in it. But this isn't a history tome and we can tell you're anxious to get to the good stuff, so we will keep it short. Until some time in the 1990s, we were in what running paleontologists called the Pre-Chipian Era. There was some overlap with the Waffle-Solian Era. There were no running chips, no chip mats at the start or finish line, no chip timing. You muscled your way to the starting line if you wanted to reduce the gap between the gun time and your starting time. You also bullied your way in front of that pig-tailed little girl in the finishing chute, even though she beat you soundly on the course, chewing bubble gum while doing it, so you could improve your finishing status.

There were fewer women back then, so the men compensated by having more hair. In running gear, you had two fabric choices: 100 percent cotton or 50/50. If you wanted ankle-length socks, you had to cut them yourself. Race directors had to compile the final times by hand, using primitive instruments like pen and paper. It could be days, even weeks, before they posted final results. Human error ruled the day. Track clubs did not have Web sites, so the results might run in the paper, but then they vanished almost as soon as they were published and were kept alive only by the oral tradition.

I know what you're thinking: That must have sucked. Why would anyone ever register for a race? But before you pass judgment on a simpler time, consider this: it was the golden age of lying about your time. You see, at every race your official time was the time on your watch. So if you "forgot" to start your watch until eight hundred meters into a 5K, there was no HAL-like starting mat to bust you. And when you mulled around the post-race fruit platters of bananas and oranges using eye contact and subtle body cues to convince your running partners that you actually beat them even though they finished minutes ahead of you, you could point to your watch and say that you started several minutes back of the starting line. And when they said that you were actually in front of the starting line and the race director had threatened to disqualify you for a false start if you didn't back up, you could say: That wasn't me. And when they pointed out that the race only had forty people in it, so there was no way it took you six minutes to get to the start, you could retort: Anybody need a protein bar? I'm going get one out of my truck.

Now that we are firmly in the Chipian Era, where the local charity will chip time a cakewalk and all results get posted on the Web before you're back down to your resting heart rate, the golden age of lying is over. It is difficult to distinguish running apparel from ballet costumes, and they sell that stuff to men. And some of them wear it. We will leave it to you to decide if this is progress. We would point out that women now make up the majority of most race fields regardless of distance. This has caused much consternation and creative excuse making among the few sexist runners who race against, and often lose to, them.

Such is the march of history. What does the future hold? Who can say? For from the beginning, running has always been, and will continue to be, about a start line, a finish line, and a buffet line's worth of excuses, recriminations, second-guessing, some fact, and more than a little fiction in between.

The Fundamentals of Training

Do What's Right for You

Coaches all seem to reinforce the same point: you need to understand the potential and limits of your own body, your strengths and weaknesses, and tailor a training plan that makes the most of your individual talent. Don't believe it for a second. We are talking about running, not getting fitted for a bespoke suit by a Saville Row tailor. Sure, you may be unique, but let's not forget that this is America. And that means that you can be anyone you want to be and do anything you want to do, even if it all comes to a tragic end. Just look at *The Great Gatsby* or Britney Spears. In America, you can accomplish anything with hard work, discipline, dedication, inherited wealth, a lawsuit in Federal Court, a lobbying firm, and a public relations agency.

What does that mean for training? It means that what worked for others has to work for you. Especially if the others are Olympians, last year's winner of the New York City Marathon, or that local freak of nature who ran a 3:00 marathon in her ninth month of pregnancy then delivered a perfectly healthy girl in the family reunion area. (She named the baby Jocelyn, pronounced jostling.) They are no better than you, what with their genetic profile and A-list endorsements. If you want to run like an elite marathoner, you should seek out the training plans of elite marathon runners. And then just jump right into it, even if it calls for ninety- to one-hundred-mile weeks when you are used to running nine- to ten-mile weeks. You'll be running marathons in sub-2:30 in no time, and by no time we mean as soon as your doctors can find a way to put your shredded ligaments and shattered joints back together.

Faster Means Faster

Coaches will tell you that fitness improvements take time and patience. You read their books and articles and realize that it's going to take forever to reach your goals. That's how they get you. They're billing by the hour just like a Wall Street law firm. But we live in a land of "instant results now while you wait fast as seen on TV." We want immediate progress. We don't want a program requiring a commitment equivalent to the time it would take to move a cemetery. We want to stick the shovel in the ground, clip the ribbon, pose with that unemployed consultant who attends all the Chamber of Commerce functions, and start breaking ground. We don't want slow drip, we want Sanka. We want a training plan with the shelf life of milk, not the half-life of uranium.

In *The Secret Book of Running*, we espouse the "Let's get it on!" training philosophy. If you follow our plan, you will succeed faster than if you use the "Best Plan," "Ultimate Plan," "Only Plan You'll Ever Need," "Marathon Plan 9 from Outer Space," or any other plan available where fraudulent training regimens are sold. That is a fact. It is as certain as a race spectator shaking a cowbell and a runner next to you yelling, "More cowbell!"

The Body Reacts to Stress

Coaches like to talk about the concept of stress. The body reacts to stress, which means that in your training you're going to have to work the muscles at least a little bit. But if no one is looking, just go ahead and skip that part. Because everywhere else you look experts are telling you that stress reduction is the key to a healthy life. They can't both be right, can they? All this conflicting advice—it's so stressful. So when we talk about stress, we have the positive benefits of a few of those ten-yard bursts during your run (not too many, let's not get carried away). We also have the negative benefits of stress—showing up on time at the office, helping with dinner at home, talking to your children. The people in your orbit need to understand that you are in training and they need to back off. Tell them as much and watch your training improve. If you tell your boss that you missed that deadline because you spent three hours at the track, you may suddenly find yourself without the stress of a job, thus giving you twenty-four hours per day to run and recover. Your non-running friends will disappear faster than a bunny in a magic show. And if you incorporate this principle at home, your only family obligation may be to mail the monthly child support payment. And we bet there is a mailbox right next to the local track.

Specificity of Training, or the Grass Is Always Greener in the Other Corral

Specificity of training is the principle that, for maximum performance, your training should correspond to your target race. If you're training for a 5K, sooner or later you are going to have to run some fast repeats of 800, 1200, and 1600 meters. If you're training for a marathon, get ready for some long runs of two to three hours. That means that you will have to be nimble in your training, for we all know that you will have at least two different target races every month, almost always of different distances. Some of these might only be a week apart, maybe even on the same weekend, which will require either an abbreviated training plan (less than twenty-four hours) or the preferred carbon-paper style overlapping plan, where you train for two different events simultaneously. It may not be just different distances either, say a 10K followed by a marathon followed by a half-marathon followed by an ultra. In the same month. No, it will be different disciplines entirely.

In the middle of summer, we know you will gaze long-ingly at the cycling and triathlon events in your town and will want to participate, if for no other reason than to justify the purchase of an expensive wet suit, time-trial bicycle, and one of those helmets worn by Death Star engineers. You will want to compete in those multi-sport events, even though in your bones you know it's a form of sports adultery, and so to atone you will also register for a steady stream of 5Ks and 10Ks. To adhere to the specificity of training principle, you will have to change your training plan the way we rec-ommend changing technical underwear: Weekly, whether it needs it or not. For the only way to get to the start line con-fidently on Saturday is to start a comprehensive, targeted training program the previous Monday.

You might ask: Wouldn't it be better to target only two to three major races per year and to train specifically for them? If you took this approach, you could incorporate several weeks of base training, then core training to improve your speed, stamina, and endurance, followed by a taper and then the race, after which you would have a recovery phase before tackling the next challenge. Wouldn't that give you the best chance to run well?

Of course it would, but you're talking twelve, sixteen, eighteen weeks or more between races. In that time, you'd miss out on a half dozen or more meaningless local races. Your friends will be wearing their cool race T-shirts and you won't have one. Can you live with that? We didn't think so. That's why we're going to hit it hard Monday through Friday, race on Saturday, then start looking down the road to next weekend. If you have been diagnosed with attention deficit disorder, you will have no trouble with this concept.

Duration Versus Distance

Someone once said that the body does not understand distance, that it only understands duration and effort. Ten miles on a flat road is different on the body than ten miles on undulating trails. Twelve miles on a forty-degree morning is different than twelve miles on a seventy-five-degree morning. If you follow that logic, and the physiology behind it is probably unassailable, then it would follow logically that your training runs, especially your long runs, would be based on duration, not distance. So if you were training for a marathon, you would gradually increase your long runs from, say, two hours to three hours. You would not be tethered to a fixed distance. Think about how liberating that would be. You would no longer have to map out a course beforehand. You would have the freedom to explore your town, to cut down that street to see where it leads. You would have no incentive to go out too fast, to "get 'er done," because you would have a fixed time to run. Two hours is two hours, whether you're running six-minute miles or nine-minute miles.

Another noted expert, whose name is lost to history, offered this advice: Omit needless miles. Smart marathon training is precise. A training program should contain no unnecessary miles, for the same reason that a runner should have no unnecessary limbs or a course no unnecessary distance. The exact mileage for optimal race performance will vary from runner to runner and can be determined through trial and error. It does not mean that all runs should be short, only that all runs have a specific purpose. For the average runner, a week should contain a long run, a "speed" workout, and the balance in easy or recovery runs. Confident runners can facilitate this goal by switching from a miles-based to a minutes-based program. The runner's goal must be to perform each workout well, not to hit a predetermined numerical goal.

These theories sound logical. They sound reasonable. But they are un-American and your internal governor (to be discussed in a future chapter) will never accept it. As long as he is in charge, the bill to convert from distance to duration will never get out of committee. It will never come up for a vote. If it is passed by a majority vote, he will veto it. It will never become law. A duration-based plan will never fly for the same reason that professional soccer can't gain real traction in the USA. Because it's part of a Socialist Plot! It just doesn't feel right. It's like the Rhythm Method—it may work but let someone else try it. We're not brave enough.

We want miles. We want that twenty-miler on the schedule. If we jog for close to four hours on an eight-degree, ninety-percent humidity morning on a course with six thousand feet of elevation change, and get back to the car with 19.75 showing on our watch, we are going to do a couple of loops around the parking lot, no matter how goofy it looks, until the odometer hits 20. No one wants to hear that the "duration" method would be better for us, that it would reduce the risk of injury, that it would prevent over-training. We want what we want. And what we want is miles.

Overtraining

Is it possible to overtrain? Is it possible to over-love or over-pray or overcoat? All these admonitions about the perils of overtraining have a secret agenda, and it's not to keep you healthy. It's to keep you down. Keep you slow. Keep you under the cushioned heel of the man. And by man I mean the SCOCATs and That Runner they are assisting. Think about your all-time best race. Remember how fast you were? Now just imagine how much faster you could have been had you trained one more mile. Just one more measly mile and you could have finished thirty seconds faster. You know this. Now imagine how much faster you would have been had you trained ten more miles. Or twenty. Or thirty. Don't fall for the argument that quality is more important than quantity. Quantity is quality, whether we're talking fries, Flintstone vitamins, or fartleks, and if you're not supersizing your mileage, if you're not doing "Biggie Workouts," you are selling yourself short. They are the best value, after all. In your bones, you know this is true. Even if those bones happen to be your shins and they're on fire right now because you took your own advice.

/ / /

The Runner's Body

The Internal Governor

People want to understand the biology and physiology behind running. We want to know what is going on inside the body that causes us to run fast or slow, to rumble along like a Greyhound bus that failed its brake inspection, or to sputter to a halt like a different greyhound bus that had its fuel line cut at the last inner-city bus station. Most trainers will try to obfuscate the issue by talking about heart rate and VO2Max, fast twitch this, slow twitch that, mitochondrial connections, and runner's hiccups. Sure, that may be what's going on at the front of the stage, but here's what's going on behind the curtain:

There is a little person inside your body. We are not making this up. In *The Lore of Running* and other major treatises on the subject, they call him the internal governor, although that is probably not entirely accurate because "governor" suggests an elected official. And we both know that you did not elect him, nor can you vote him out of office—not even with one of those "cleansing" programs that are advertised on the radio. Some runners find it difficult to accept that there's a little person inside them, but it's true. If you don't believe me, go get a sonogram. Go on, men. I'm sure your health plan covers it.

What does he look like? Sort of like Ben Kingsley in *Schindler's List*. He has wire-rim glasses and one of these green eyeshades that accountants wore in the 1920s. He sits at a desk on your right-hand side. He keeps a copy of your training schedule on that desk. He monitors you. He sees you when you're sleeping. He knows when you're awake. And if you deviate from your plan so much as a step, he will punish you. He may look like Gandhi, but he's a curmudgeon like Larry David. Ever wonder where side stitches come from? You guessed it. He doesn't even have to get up from his desk to cause one. He simply pulls a lever on the left.

Fairly or not, the internal governor can be a real tyrant. He's grumpy. It's dark in there, rather damp, and he doesn't get out much—well, ever. He will not hesitate to sabotage you. Do not provoke him. Skip a workout, and you can be sure he will get you down the road. Do the workout but cut it short (because, for instance, your daughter is being rushed to the hospital for an appendectomy) and he will bide his time then cut *you* short. He demands respect, he demands deference, he demands absolute fidelity to that training plan. If you do not follow that plan to the letter, you are asking for it, just as sure as if you wing it through a yeast bread recipe. That boule will not rise and neither will you. From shin splints to chronic fatigue, IT band issues to a bad case of the vapors, there's nothing he can't do or cause.

If you show him the proper respect, however, he just might reward you. He could press the "runner's high" button (two switches below the side-stitch lever). Rarer still, if you nail eighteen weeks of training perfectly, the equivalent of maximizing your campaign contributions, getting down on bended knee to kiss the ring, and presenting him with a burnt offering, he might flip the "negative split" and "personal record" levers simultaneously. But don't expect that every weekend or even every year. Mostly, he is a miserable old codger looking for any excuse to stick it to you.

The Cardiovascular System

Doctors will tell you that the cardiovascular system—the heart and the system of vessels that transport blood (and by extension, oxygen) to the running muscles—is a critical component to running success. They will also say that a runner's ultimate potential is, to a great degree, predetermined by the power and efficiency of the cardiovascular system. But they are paid to say that. It can't be that we are saddled with random biological baggage. If you can't keep up with that lithe runner in the neighborhood, it's not because your heart is too small. It's because you don't have one. Because you don't want it bad enough. You're not trying hard enough. Sure, you may be getting up before work to run, but are you also running in the afternoon, even if it means jeopardizing your job or leaving little Johnny alone in the car line? We didn't think so. So don't blame it on your cardiovascular system. Take the example of the Tin Man and go get a new heart.

Physical Setbacks

In the past, you have put in your training, watched your diet, and peaked with the timing of a blooming azalea bed at The Masters. Then you ran your race, and when you looked down at your watch, it read the exact time you had hoped to run. Unfortunately, you were doubled-over at an aid station four miles from the finish line. And leading up to race day, you did everything right. Your time is an aberration and an abomination. What happened? The logical explanation is that somewhere along the way you crossed your internal governor, and he is paying you back the Lyndon B. Johnson way.

But that may not be the only explanation. For the internal governor gets the benefit of law and is innocent until proven guilty. If the internal governor is not to blame, then there is only one other possibility—the running gods are punishing you. Not because you took ten dollars from the offertory plate. No, God is punishing you because That Runner, in some twisted voodoo-meets-expo ritual, laid out offerings to the running gods so you would falter. Maybe she sacrificed a chicken, maybe it was just a nice pair of socks. It doesn't matter. She built an altar, sprinkled it with Gatorade, squirted and smeared gel on some printed race results, and prayed for you to run thirty seconds per mile slower than you are capable. She probably made a little voodoo doll of you, using a sneaker ball or an old chip for your head and impaling you with bib pins.

How do we suggest you deal with setbacks? You should curse the gods. Then you should pray to those same gods for payback. For even the SCOCATs will attest that the gods rarely take sides. They are suckers for a desperate runner with a shiny altar.

A Remembrance of Runs Past—Advice for Older Runners

Youth is wasted on the young, and so are fast race times. Many of you reading this book are coming to running for the first time in your late twenties, thirties, forties, or later. But some of you are coming back to running after a long layoff for college, career, or seven to ten years of hard labor with no possibility of parole. (If you're the guy who ran *The Jericho Mile*, this section does not apply to you.) And those runners stand in the road like Janus, one face looking at that future race on the calendar and the other looking back at past glory. For you may have had a semi-successful running career back during your Paulie Bleeker days. Maybe you ran track or cross-country. You were skinny back then, fleet of foot and fond of Ratt. You had unlimited energy…and acne. You could do the most body-destroying workout and still recover like the villain in *Terminator 2*. You could just pound it and pound it and pound it, multiple times a day. And you ran, too.

You want to recapture that youthful spirit, but more importantly, you want to run that fast again. Can it be done? Of course it can. In your first week back. You're entitled to it. It's your birthright. Like that convertible at forty. It's simple: just start doing exactly what you did when you were in high school. It worked then, so why shouldn't it work now? Run fast, run often, shotgun your recovery beverage, and apply Clearasil liberally. (Don't worry, they don't test at the local races, so your Kabuki mask will not cause a false positive.) There's no reason why you shouldn't hold the same pace on long runs that you did back then, even if you're thirty years older with a bad back. Take a long look in the mirror. Behind those crow's feet and liver spots is a smoking-fast nineteen-year old. You're not going to let that scrawny teenager get the better of you, are you?

If that doesn't work, you can either hate yourself for the pitiful excuse of a runner that you have degenerated into, or feel sorry for yourself. We recommend both, switching off day by day so your mood will always catch your spouse off guard. Depending on how good you were as a kid and how far you have fallen in midlife, you may find yourself refusing to race at all, incapable of bearing the sight of your slow time when you cross the finish line. Some people might consider such an approach unhealthy, even irrational. But it is not. It is the appropriate, indeed, the only response because you are unique, and the immutable laws of aging do not apply to you. Your inability to train or race at your high school or college level has nothing to do with the aging of your body. Rather, it is a personal failing exacerbated by the lack of adequate support from your spouse, children, priest, and colleagues.

So, how do we put these principles together into a cohesive training plan? We're about to tell you.

/ / /

Training with the JAR Method

You will never hear coaches admit it, but there is only one surefire program for running success. It's called the JAR Method. JAR stands for jealousy, anger, and resentment. Forget about positive mental attitude. Forget about just enjoying the journey. Those platitudes never earned anyone a third place in their age group. And forget supplements and special diets and that funny-smelling cream that the guy at the Y is always trying to sell you. (That can't be legal, can it? Can men actually sell Avon?) You've heard of going to the well? Well, forget that, unless there's a baby down there, in which case get over there and call 9-1-1 and CNN. Don't go the well, go to the JAR. You need only put these three arrows in your quiver, and then you need to train those arrows on the bull's-eye on the back of That Runner. Now, we're speaking metaphorically here. We know what some of you are thinking, but we don't want you to go out like you're Legolas in *Lord of the Rings* and do something crazy. This book is about running, not archery.

If you're going to have a breakthrough, you need to start obsessing about That Runner the way Saliari obsessed about Mozart. We need good, old-fashioned loathing. You're going to have to seethe. You're going to have to break a Commandment. We're going to need you to covet your neighbor's wife's race times.

A training plan is like a cocktail, even if it's more like a Molotov cocktail under the JAR Method. The JAR provides the raging kinetic action to shake the cocktail into something frothy—not your mouth, if we are doing our job. But what do we put inside the shaker? Runs and workouts of varying types, which we will explain now.

Easy Runs

Easy runs are designed to help you recover from more strenuous workouts and should be done at a conversational intensity. If you are running alone, then talk to yourself; and if you struggle to hold a conversation, then you are probably running too fast. Or you're boring. If you are running with a partner, then the intensity should be adjusted and readjusted so that you are always running slightly faster than your partner. The "conversational" aspect of the pace need be limited to your ability to pant, "You doing OK back there?" or, if your partner gets ahead of you: "Do you mind slowing down? What do you think this is—a race?"

Long Runs

The long run is the cornerstone of every marathon training program. You may also know it as the death march or the slog. It's those Saturday or Sunday mornings of two, three, or four hours on your feet. We put them in the program so you will have multiple opportunities to change your mind about the race. It always seems to be an even number you're after: fourteen, sixteen, eighteen, or twenty miles. Odd numbers, especially large prime numbers like seventeen and nineteen, never get targeted. The long run also provides the runner training for the marathon with several chances to practice going out too fast and walking the final few miles.

Tempo Runs

Tempo runs and threshold runs are speed workouts of anywhere between ten to thirty minutes and designed to be run at a comfortably hard pace. A tempo run is slightly slower, at a dry heave and dizzy pace, about the pace of a 1985 Ford Tempo at full speed. A threshold run is at full-blown vomit pace. The runner is encouraged to do the entire workout as close as possible to the prescribed speed. In other words, you should run as fast as you can for three to five minutes, then hold your side and walk or jog for the rest of the workout.

Intervals

Intervals are like threshold runs except there are more of them. On the one hand, the distance is shorter. On the other hand, there are more of them. You get a short break between each interval, which gives you multiple opportunities to bag the speed session. As with other speed workouts, you should try to set the Olympic record on the first interval so that you can barely walk through the remaining intervals.

Hill Repeats

You can't spell *hell* without *hill*. Wait a second, you can. Let me start over. Hill repeats are a form of training where, believe it or not, a runner will voluntarily run up a steep incline over and over. Hill repeats provide all the pain, nausea, and light-headedness of a track session, only in slow motion. If you are going to incorporate hill repeats into your training plan, you will need to find two hills—the one you tell people you run and the one you actually run. The former should have a name (something like Deadman's Grade) and be part of the town lore. It helps if the hill was responsible for an *Ethan Frome*–like sledding tragedy. As for the hill you actually run, any nearby pitcher's mound will do.

Fartlek

Fartlek, it's the workout that makes you snicker. The word has no real meaning. The SCOCATs made up that word just to see how many people would actually say it. It's one thing to write it, but actually to say it out loud? It's painful and embarrassing at the same time—just like our prom experience. Some will say that the word means "speedplay" in Swedish. They made that up too. If fartlek means speedplay, then Abba means cruise intervals. No, if you want to do a run that incorporates random bursts of speed of varying intensity efforts and duration, don't say you're going out for a fartlek (especially if you're telling it to that new girl you've been out with only once). No, just say you're going out for a run that incorporates random bursts of speed of varying intensity efforts and durations. Wait, that is a mouthful. We need to come up with a name for that. Yes, instead of calling it a fartlek, tell her you're going for a belchie. That has a much more elegant sound to it.

Walking

As much as it pains us to admit it, walking is the new easy run. We have come to appreciate it as a "no pain, all gain" workout. We encourage fifty to sixty minutes of walking every Sunday. Sunday walks are an ideal way to remedy aches and cramps and get the blood circulating in your legs. It will prepare you for the Monday workout.

We recommend you take these walks at a local park with a well-trafficked loop trail. Midway through our walk, you might stumble upon a family of deer. As you stop to watch them eat, you may soon learn that not everyone on the trail wants to commune with nature. A guy in cut-off jeans and a fanny pack might walk by, cell phone to his ear, yammering away. As he passes, you may hear him say, "Some guy never seen a deer before." Then two women may come by, and when you whisper excitedly, "Deer!" and point, one (of the women) might respond, "We don't care." "Did you care when they killed Bambi's mother, you %$%#@!" you might whisper back. For the rest of the walk, your son might be subjected to a rambling, impassioned lecture on what Mark Twain called the "damned human race." This is just one completely hypothetical possibility for your Sunday walk.

Rest

We have no use for rest. Coaches will tell you that ample rest is a critical part of training. They will say that it is during rest that the body adapts and improves. But if the body improves and adapts during rest, then many of us should already be Olympic-caliber runners. We rested for years, after all, before we took up running. So that theory cannot be correct. Besides, if you take time off, That Runner will gain on you.

Embrace the Treadmill

Trainers say that you're selling yourself short if you run on the treadmill. We don't think so. They say it's easier to run on the treadmill than on the road. We don't think so. (They may be right if you leave the incline at 0 percent. That's why we encourage you to treat your easy treadmill runs like our preferred restaurant tip—1 percent.) They say that you won't be able to race fast if you spend too much time on the treadmill. We. Don't. Think. So.

Most of the SCOCATs will recoil and make a face like you just opened a post-Katrina refrigerator when you use the *t* word. But no less an authority than Jack Daniels of "Daniels' Running Formula" encourages running on the treadmill, so if you need a higher authority to green-light your treadmills, there it is. For us, the treadmill is not just for laundry anymore. We believe a treadmill is key as much out of necessity as anything else. It is the ultimate baby-sitter if you have a working spouse and your choices are either run at home on a treadmill, preferably with the treadmill and child both within "don't put your hand in the blender!" distance, or don't run at all.

We acknowledge that a treadmill can turn you into something of a Goldilocks runner—only running outside if the weather is just right. But in a half-marathon or marathon training program, you have only so much mental capital in the bank. Every time you have to go out and run in the cold or the rain or the dark, or all three, particularly in the winter, you have to make a withdrawal from the bank. If you have to do that three to four times per week over eighteen weeks, eventually your account is going to be as bankrupt as Lehman Brothers. We would rather you use the treadmill on nasty days, or in a scheduling pinch, and save the mental capital.

The treadmill can also be a track substitute. If you are not comfortable on the track but like (or better yet, need) speedwork and the results of speedwork, use the treadmill. We hate going to the track because you have to *go* to the track. We would rather just go to our basement. If it's a workout where the repeats are a mile or less, you can do them on the treadmill. And you know you will be running them at the exact pace prescribed, neither too fast or too slow. Another great thing about the treadmill is that if the pace is too fast, just get off and the treadmill will finish the workout for you. How great is that? Our treadmill once did a twenty-miler and ten 4-minute miles in the same week, while we painted a room and braised a pot roast.

Finally, the treadmill allows you to multitask by running and catching up on your favorite TV shows. For a hard tempo run on the treadmill, nothing beats C-SPAN. And for those vomit-inducing 1200-meter repeats, we recommend something from the Food Network. One word of caution: if you have a shaky equilibrium or lose balance easily, best to avoid all Tour de France coverage, where one too many of those motorcycle-camera shots will have you catapulted into the back wall in no time.

So when it comes to treadmills, forget what you may have heard and listen to your internal governor, who has this to say: embrace your inner hamster. And to do so, here are some treadmill-specific workouts. Remember to remove all drying clothing from the treadmill before you begin.

Boiling the Frog—You have heard the saying that you don't boil a frog by dropping him in boiling water, because he will hop out. Instead, you drop him in cool water and gradually increase the heat. This workout is similar, and yes, you are the frog. Only that's not your princess kissing you if you get carried away and find yourself on your back at the YMCA. That's an emergency medical technician and she's administering CPR. To do the workout, start at a low pace and gradually increase every couple of minutes until you are "boiling."

Ascent of Mount Everest—Everyone agrees that hill training will make you a stronger runner. So imagine what mountain training will do for you. Set the incline to 10 percent. Set the pace to 10 MPH. Step on the treadmill. When you wake up in your hospital bed, promise your spouse you will never try that again.

The Conflicted Foodie—You will need a television with cable for this one. Set the treadmill to a comfortable pace and incline. Turn the TV to the Food Network. Jog and plan what you will eat as soon as you finish your workout.

The New Father—Get on the treadmill. Warm up for five minutes. Uh-oh, the baby is crying. Stop. Go upstairs. Rock the baby. Come back down. Warm up for two more minutes then run for one minute at goal pace. Can you believe it? The baby is crying again. Stop. Go upstairs. Rock the baby. Come back down. One minute at goal pace. Jeez, what is that baby's problem? He's doing this on purpose. Stop. Go upstairs. Rock the baby. Tell him, "This is it!" Run at pace for four to five minutes while baby cries. Ignore the crying. Fail to realize that your wife just walked into the house. (This workout can't be repeated since your wife is likely to burn the treadmill.)

Reversal of Fortune—Set the treadmill to an easy jog pace. Get on backwards and run backwards. Pretend that someone is running in front of you and say things like "Come on! Pick it up? You're only about twenty minutes behind my time!" This is the perfect workout for those marathoners who insist on going back out on the course after they finish so they can "run you in."

Putting Your Plan Together

Under the JAR Method of training, you will incorporate all of the above workouts into your schedule. You will also use the treadmill as necessary. We have developed a precise, scientifically proven, foolproof method for creating training plans that will fit you better than your best pair of jeans. Here is how it works: you are going to need three six-sided dice. I hope you purchased your set of authentic *Secret Book of Running* dice and have them ready to roll now. If not, it's time to get Yahtzee off the shelf. You will also need a pair of scissors, some scrap paper, a bowl, a pencil, and a blank calendar. Do you have everything? Good, then let's get started.

Your program will run anywhere from three to eighteen weeks, as determined by the dice roll. Go ahead and roll. Wait! Don't forget to blow on them for good luck. Now! Luck be a lady tonight! Let's consider your number. If it's three, you will have your work cut out for you. But the outcome of your roll is clearly God's will, so you'll just have to make it work for you. As the Soup Nazi might say, if he sold training plans instead of mulligatawny, no taper for you! Take your blank calendar and circle your target race date. Now work backwards twenty-one days from that date. That will be your training cycle.

Grab that piece of paper and write the name of each workout on it. Now use the scissors to cut out the name of each workout. Put those strips in the bowl. Put the bowl over your head and pick one. No peeking. What does it say? Long run? Guess what you're doing on Day 1 of your workout. Long run. I suggest fifteen. Write it on the calendar. Put the strip back in the bowl. Pick again. Long run again?! Tough draw. But make it work for you and go for twenty. Continue drawing until you have picked for all twenty-one days of your cycle. Take a look at your customized calendar. If that doesn't get you qualified for Boston, nothing will.

But, you may ask, what if I roll three but my race is more than three weeks away? Then pick another event, silly.

These are only the running workouts in the JAR system. We also encourage a healthy dose of cross-training. On at least three, preferably seven, days of the week, we would like you to spend at least an hour obsessing about That Runner. Do it until you sweat. Remember, no pain, no gain. One workout could be given over to brooding, while another could be spent fantasizing about some tragic mishap befalling him or her. You could spend one day making a list and diagrams of ways to sabotage her, or at the other extreme you could sit in quiet contemplation of how sick he makes you. Some of our runners have found success with a circuit training approach, where they do equal sets of stewing, sulking, and chafing, with a recovery mope between each set.

Feel free to be creative. The key is to find some post-running time each week to really stoke the flames of the JAR bonfire so that it is raging come race day.

Race Distances

Most runners have a variety of local race distances to choose from, from one-mile fun runs (where the competition is usually ten and under) to the marathon and beyond. Each distance has its advantages and disadvantages, its charms and its challenges. We compiled the following information on the most common race distances.

5K—The 5K is 3.1 miles long. The .1 was added by the SCOCATs to confuse you when you try to calculate your mile pace. The 5K is the fundraiser of choice for any organization in need of money. So although the 5K is a paltry distance, only one-eighth the length of the marathon, it makes up for it in volume. If you live in a town big enough to have a local celebrity news anchor, chances are you can run forty 5Ks per year without leaving the county. And whereas the marathon spreads the pain over many miles, the 5K reduces it to its essence. It offers a more concentrated dose of suffering. If marathon pain is like a packet of Kool-Aid added to one gallon of water, the 5K is that same packet added to one cup of water. In case you're wondering about the flavor, it is red.

10K—The 10K is 6.2 miles long. Coaches call it the perfect marriage of speed and distance. But really, is there such a thing as a perfect marriage? This is more of an arranged marriage, and a doomed one at that. It's the "Kramer Versus

Kramer" of race distances. Somebody didn't speak up, and all runners are now required to forever hold their piece. Runners, in their infinite wisdom, will usually attack the 10K with a strategy of running their 5K pace and then "holding on" to the end. They start holding at 3.2 and by 3.3 miles realize that, like some of those passengers on the railing in *Titanic*, they are not going to be able to hold on much longer. Only they don't fall into the Atlantic. Instead, they slow to a walk, giving them ample time to reflect that with the 10K, after you run 3.1 miles, you have to run another 3.1 miles.

Half-marathon—The half-marathon is 13.1 miles long. It is the race distance with an identity crisis. There are no half-football games or half-tennis matches. In golf, you may only play nine holes, but you stopped not because the match was over but because it started raining or the clubhouse manager discovered that you're not a member of the club. The half-marathon is saddled with that unfortunate, negative qualifier. It would be such a proud distance were it called a 21K, which sounds bold and powerful. No one is going to give 21K a wedgie when he walks down the hall. But the half is getting tossed into the trash and its house is egged regularly. And perhaps that is why it takes out its frustrations on runners. For although it is half of the marathon, it remains a full 13.1 miles. That gives it plenty of room to get medieval on unprepared and cocky runners who go in thinking: *It's just a half.*

Marathon. The marathon is 26.2 miles long. It's the big one, the itch that must be scratched. If the 5K is a sitcom, the 10K a drama, and the half-marathon a "Movie of the Week," then the marathon is a mini-series. It's *The Thorn-birds* with singlets instead of clerical garb. It requires the most preparation, not only with training but also with compiling information about the race to share with every person with which you come into contact. It is the longest of the classic (read: non-freak) race distances. It has the most water stops (except in Chicago that one time), usually the largest crowds, and sometimes the coolest finisher's medal. Some runners say the marathon is a jealous mistress. But that is not accurate. The marathon is a jealous husband who is a psychopathic ex-SEAL and current cage fighter who just learned you're fooling around with his wife. In both situations—signing up for the marathon or dating the wife—the same rationale applies: "It seemed like a good idea at the time."

At 26.2 miles, the marathon is a long, grueling race that requires a unique approach to training and racing. The marathon does not abide mistakes that you can get away with in a 5K, 10K, or half-marathon. Your training is different, your fueling is different, and your race strategy is different. It is critical, therefore, for you to recognize the uniqueness of the race so you can attack it appropriately. The marathon is, after all, the only race that counts for most runners. And that tantalizing personal record or Boston-qualifying time waits at the finish line. So here are a few race-day tips to guarantee a breakout marathon performance:

1. Set the right time goal. After your four- to forty-week training program, with its variety of races at shorter distances, you will have a good sense of how fast you can run at different distances. You can take those numbers and use one of several Internet calculators to estimate or "predict" your ideal mara-

thon goal pace. For instance, one common rule of thumb is to take your half-marathon time, double it, then add ten minutes to get your marathon time. Once you have that projected pace, go ahead and ignore it. In all likelihood, it is not as fast as it needs to be to meet your marathon goal. Who cares if that projected pace is "logical" or "grounded in reality" or "your best chance at avoiding a DNF?" You may not have been able to break twenty-five minutes in a 5K last month, but that's no reason why you can't go sub-3:00 in the marathon. You just need to run that pace as long as your legs will allow and then "gut it out" to the finish line. It doesn't matter if you never ran a step at that pace during your training. Why waste your marathon performance on a mere weekend long run? Just because all your long runs were at 9:00/mile pace doesn't mean you can't race at 8:00/mile pace. It's called "saving energy," dude! Fast times are about heart, after all. So, for marathon success, we consider it best to subtract anywhere from ten to thirty seconds off that projected per mile pace. Go ahead and wear the faster pace band to reinforce your decision. It's marathon day, after all, a day when the immutable realities of fitness and physiology don't apply, and a runner—if she clicks her heels three times and believes it fiercely enough—can accomplish anything.

2.   Save time by skipping the water stops. Race directors will station water stops at every mile or so on the course. They are there to distract the runners. Smart racers know that they can save five, six, maybe seven seconds per mile if they just skip them. But won't that leave me dehydrated later in the race, you may wonder? Maybe, but think of all the time you will have "put in the bank." You'll have plenty of time to quench your thirst once the race is over. The key is to get to the finish line before

you dehydrate. Again, you may have to "gut it out" for the last, say, twenty miles, but that's what the marathon is all about. You will outrun your thirst.

3. Surprise! I'm your pre-race meal! Coaches will say that you should standardize your pre-race meal and eat it over and over in training. Nothing could be further from the truth. If you do that, your body will become accustomed to that same, bland breakfast. It will take it for granted. It will have a sense of entitlement and expectation. It's your body calling: "I'm ready for my bagel and banana." That is not the way you want to start a race. No, on race morning, you want to shock the system. You want to show your body who is in charge. So give it some bacon or some grillade and grits. Don't be afraid to feed it scrapple or hash or eggs Benedict. That will teach it a lesson. Your body will respect you for it. And then, when the starting gun sounds, your body will be ready to serve its master.

Monitoring Your Progress

At *The Secret Book of Running*, we strongly recommend that you keep a running journal. A journal is a valuable tool for monitoring your progress. You can do this at some Web sites, but nothing beats a paper calendar, notebook, and three-ring binder. If you're going to do it right, you will need to record more than your daily mileage. While logging your mileage is a good starting point, you should also record the following about each workout and race:

- Time of day
- Pace
- Type of run

- Perceived effort
- Average heart rate
- Calories burned
- Estimated carbon footprint
- Course map with elevation chart
- Weather (temperature, conditions, UV index, wind, barometric pressure)
- Fluids and food consumed during run
- Summary of all thoughts during run (See the section on running with a hand-held recorder.)
- The Dow Jones Industrial Average at start and finish
- A short poem or bit of doggerel describing the run
- No less than six pictures taken before, during, and after the run
- A description of the clothing you wore for the run (in case something happens to the pictures)
- The name of That Runner you obsessed about during the run, in keeping with the JAR Method

You should compile, color-code, and cross-reference all this information using a variety of graphs and pie charts. You should put all of this information in a three-ring binder, carry it with you at all times, and study it assiduously. The people around you want you to share this information with them, and there is nothing wrong in doing so. We encourage you to read your entries at the dinner table, during church services, and in the elevator.

///

Nutrition and Hydration

Nutrition

At *The Secret Book of Running*, we get asked the same question over and over: Now that I'm a runner, can I eat whatever I want? After all, as the saying goes, if the furnace is hot enough, it will burn anything. We caution against taking that advice too literally. First, let's be honest. If you're running thirty miles per week or less, you're furnace is not that hot. You are not forging steel. You are not making glass. You might be able to turn a marshmallow beige over five to seven minutes. The other thing about this furnace analogy—are you eating coal or wood? If so, you really need to reduce your dependence on fossil fuels. Besides, they are not filled with carbohydrates.

That gets us to carbohydrates. And you can't talk about carbohydrates without talking about carbo-loading. At *The Secret Book of Running*, we believe many runners get into running at least in part for the carbo-loading. It's their license to fill. After all, if you're going to run three miles, you really need to eat a pound of pasta the night before. And on the night before the marathon, we would rather not conjure up the image of bottomless-binging that occurs at "Pasta Parties" across the nation. But we will tell you that we know a guy who became independently wealthy by buying Olive Garden stock the night before the New York City Marathon.

Carbohydrates are good. They are necessary. You should develop a lasting, long-term relationship with bagels and your nut butter of choice. But don't forget about protein. Recovering muscles don't need carbohydrates. They need protein. Pancakes are great before a run, or during, but after a long run, consider the egg.

If cholesterol is an issue, don't eat eggs. But if it isn't, why wouldn't you jump at an excuse to eat them three to four days per week? They're incredible and edible. And you have to love the packaging. These days, in most towns you can get them from a local farm where the chickens play backgammon and gin rummy all day. You will find that unlike factory eggs, these yolks are velvety and divine. When you're not having a couple of eggs sunny side up, over easy, poached, scrambled, shirred, or as an omelet, you should try a slab of smoked salmon. It's more expensive than eggs, but a delicious start to the morning. It's a clean protein that is loaded with long-chain omega 3s, the same material used to make expensive Swiss watches.

Salmon and eggs are the A-listers, and for supporting roles, have a piece of whole-grain toast and a small bowl of fruit, yogurt, and raw almonds. When feeling frisky, try a squirt of honey. It makes for a colorful table. It requires a little effort, but if you can bang out your morning workout, then fix this breakfast, you are ready for anything the day will bring.

Or you can just carbo-load and eat eight waffles.

There's nothing wrong with bread and pasta. We love bread at *The Secret Book of Running*, we put the local Artisan Bread Festival on our calendar six months in advance, and our death-row meal would probably be hot French bread and syrup. We like pasta, too. Pasta is perfect for the night before a long run, but for the rest of the week you probably don't need it. Every meal need not look like something that would cause Dr. Atkins to strangle himself with some al dente tagliatelle. Unless your training plan calls for two or more long runs each week, you need only carbo-load one night per week—the night before your long run. The rest of the week, you can push the protein, which will help repair your muscles and will keep you lean and hard. A pound or two less, and a little more lean muscle on your frame, and you can easily shave off a few seconds per mile in your next marathon.

If your body craves red meat, eat it. Sometimes that yearning for red meat is the body's signal that it needs and wants iron. Sometimes it's the internal governor telling you it just won't work out with that vegan from accounting. There is nothing wrong with a hamburger made from local, grass-fed ground beef. Or a steak for that matter. Are there less fatty alternatives? Absolutely. But will a steak kill your chances at Boston glory? Absolutely not. Fries and a milkshake have no business in any training plan, except that if you're going to run forty miles per week or more and train hard, it would be a crime not to have fries and ice cream once per week. You are a runner, not a monk.

Let's talk about coffee. We drink it every morning, have since we were kids and our mother served it the way Harvey Keitel liked it in *Pulp Fiction*—lots of cream and lots of sugar. But we never used to drink it on race morning. We always had a cup or two before long runs to wake up and warm up. We were afraid to drink it on race day because caffeine is a diuretic. (Diuretic, from the Latin, for dude on the side of the road half a mile into a race.) Well, it turns out the risk of dehydration is over-hyped. Further, it turns out that caffeine can be a powerful, natural performance-enhancing drug. The scientific consensus is that caffeine improves race performance at all distances. The exercise physiologists reached this conclusion when they noticed that six of the top ten all-time performances in the marathon are held by a runner named Mr. Coffee. If you are a coffee drinker, you should drink coffee. Why deny your body something it has come to expect every other day of the year on race day?

If you drink tea, we have no recommendation for you. Go back to England, you embracer of the metric system.

So, in summary, to fuel your body, add these items to your next grocery bill: eggs, smoked salmon, beef, and coffee.

When it comes to good sources of carbohydrates, a guiding principle is: if it's brown, wolf it down. Remember, as your in-laws never fail to mention, you are not refined. Your food should not be refined either. Brown grains, wheat pasta, dark breads, or a shredded paper bag (in a salad) are all good choices. On the subject of grains, we know you prefer white rice. We do, too. It's fluffier. But brown rice is better, even if it gets caught in your teeth. So start buying it. You'll probably want to start cooking it now if your target race is three weeks away, since it takes about that time to cook. Rice is not the only grain available to the runner search for nutritious energy. Couscous, Israeli or otherwise, is a good choice. So is quinoa, the new couscous, and a favorite among runners who also play Scrabble. Some people swear by bulgur, but we couldn't get anyone on the editorial staff to try it so you're on your own with that one. Any food that sounds like a cross between vulgar and burlap can't be good.

You also need to switch to whole-wheat pasta. It's healthier. Now when it comes to pasta shapes, this is vitally important. If you're training for a half-marathon to a marathon, you want to eat spaghetti, linguine, or fettuccine. If you are training for anything shorter, go with rigatoni, penne, or elbow macaroni. Under no circumstances should you use orecchiette or tagliatelle. Don't ask why. Just trust us on this one. With bread, if you go to your local heath-food store and loaf around the bakery—get it? loaf around—you will find a variety of options to pick from. Go with anything that looks like it would not be out of place on the table of a peasant in any Russian novel from the nineteenth century. If you see a loaf that looks like it could double as a bird feeder because of all the seeds in the crust, that's the one you want to buy and eat. If they don't have any seedy bread—and make sure you ask the stock clerks for the seedy bread—go with anything that includes cracked wheat, oats, barley, or rye.

What about breakfast cereals? If you have to ask, you can't have it. Lucky Charms are out. Count Chocula never finished a 5K, and although Froot Loops may sound like it's associated with the track, we can assure you that it is not. On the hot side, oatmeal is good for you, particularly if you spike it with dried fruit or nuts (almonds or walnuts, to be precise), instead of enough brown sugar and cinnamon to supply the local Cinnabon. If you're from the South, you are probably wondering about grits. We love grits, but you know what they call grits made without copious amounts of butter and cream—mortar. Best to save them for after your training cycle. On the cold side, you can experiment with different brands. What you're looking for something in the granola family, something made with whole grains and supplement with bran or fiber or both, something in quarry-grade clumps that will scoff when you pour milk over it. In fact, that is a good test for your cold cereal. Pour some in a bowl. Pour milk over it. Go study abroad for a semester. Come back. Is the cereal soggy? If so, toss it out. If not, you are buying the right cereal for your next marathon.

If you stray past the bakery and into the frozen foods aisle, right next to the organic frozen waffles you might find what we call Bible bread. These are the frozen bagels, rolls, buns, and loaves made from "sprouted" wheat. What does sprouted mean? Excellent question. Apparently, instead of starting the baking process with a bag of flour, these bakers (We could also insert hippie scientists) nurture wheat berries in water until they sprout to life and begin to grow. They are then mercilessly slaughtered and ground into a mushy dough. That dough becomes the basis for the bread. This is how they did it in biblical times. We're sure you have heard the phrase: "Man cannot live on bread alone." But do you know the rest of it? The full sentence is "Man cannot live on bread alone. Unless it's sprouted. Pass me another sprouted slice, home slice!" In fact, some companies even reference the specific Bible passage that contains the recipe for their loaf. We would not hold ourselves out as biblical scholars, so it was with some surprise to learn that there are, in fact, recipes in the Bible. (But alas, no directions on how to turn water into wine at home.) Fortunately, this particular bread recipe is not from the Book of Revelation. Religion and technique aside, the sprouting process is supposed to make the bread healthier for your body. And what's more, if you eat at least three sprouted bagels in one day, it counts for Sunday Mass.

As for vegetables, they are all good, but if it's dark, leafy, and tough, better suited for making a thatched roof than a salad, then it's really good for you. Eat those, as well as sweet potatoes (or a regular potato dyed orange) and broccoli (because we're fans of bonsai).

A final word on nutrition. Let us ponder the schizophrenic condition that is the runner training for a marathon who also goes on a low-carb diet. This is the same person who would try to fly a kite but give up wind. Don't do it.

Hydration

When it comes to hydration, most runners, especially marathoners, tend to espouse the water-balloon strategy. On the day before and morning of the race, the goal is to see how much liquid they can consume without bursting. In so doing, by the starting gun they look less like runners and more like a Macy's Day Parade float. The runner does not so much jog as slosh out of the gate. He is bloated, he desperately needs to urinate, and he has put himself at risk for hyponatremia. But he won't be dehydrated.

This thirsty runner does not trust the race director either. Though promised fluids at every mile, this runner will have that parachute-with-a-feeding-tube contraption on his back—just in case. He will wear the bandolier-like FuelBelt. He will be two-fisted with water bottles. He would run with a garden hose if he could find one 26.2 miles long. He will likely empty every receptacle by the first mile and refill everything at the first aid station. He will repeat this twenty-six times. He will finish two hours beyond his goal and ten pounds heavier than when he started and tell his wife: "I would have qualified for Boston but I think I got dehydrated out there."

Of course, this strategy is not necessary to avoid dehydrating during a marathon. It is a marathon, after all, not a desert crossing. The runner should save the supersizing for his trips to McDonald's where she will gain extra "value" (to say nothing of calories) by slurping those extra gallons. For a marathon or half-marathon, a little extra Gatorade the day before and on race morning is all you need. During the race, a cup at every aid station should suffice, two if it's a hot day.

///

Adversity in All Its Guises

Don't Let the Miracle of Life Interfere with Your Training Schedule

In any training program, you will have to deal with adversity, be it injury, bad weather, or the birth of a child. You can't do much about the first two, but they invented the jogging stroller to deal with the third. An interesting factoid about the jogging stroller: always the most pristine piece of used sporting-good equipment at any secondhand shop. With a decent jogging stroller, there's no reason why "the miracle of life" should affect your schedule. We believe the children are our future and that their future is in a jogging stroller.

Consider this testimonial:

Dear Secret Book of Running:

The scene would have made Thoreau climb out of his Barcalounger, engage his TIVO, and take notice through the window. The frosty morning mist rose off the pond—not Walden Pond, not Golden Pond, just the pond—like steam on a cup of tea microwaved for too long. Three Canadian geese glided single-file along the far bank. The lead goose honked to the others, as if to say, "Where's the guy with the stale bread?" The second goose responded, "I wish he'd bring some whole wheat. All that sourdough has me fatter than—well—fatter than a Christmas goose." To which the third added, "Maybe that's the point. You see any 'No Hunting' signs, you moron?"

Leaves mail-ordered from L.L. Bean drizzled down softly, like balloons at a political convention, only they were flat and leaf-shaped and not made of rubber or inflated or tied in a knot at the end. In the clearing, a mother deer reviewed her doe's algebra. Somewhere, a bitter woodpecker committed libel on a cedar tree.

And there, in the distance, where the running trail came down the hill and leveled off, stood the jogging stroller, a glistening, majestic, carbon-fiber chariot. Inside sat Junior, angelic, ethereal, a mild case of diaper rash. And above him—if we allow ourselves to pause the frame—a silhouetted figure in mid-flight, horizontal and bug-eyed, hovering above the stroller like the guardian angel in Augustus St. Gauden's Shaw Memorial. That's me: the silhouette, not the angel.

It was one of those mornings where your breath scrapes its way out of your mouth before falling to the ground and shattering like a light bulb. It was cold, but nothing I couldn't handle. My extended musical career has forced me to adapt to weather extremes. The band and I have been singing around flaming fifty-gallon drums as far back as the blizzard of '93. I have tried to interest my son in this profession. I even put his little Oscar the Grouch garbage pail on the back deck and lit it on fire. Painted to resemble aluminum but on close inspection made of plastic, it melted quickly, as did my dreams of Junior joining me on the doo-wop circuit.

I am a proponent of a hole-punch method of training that is as inflexible as heavy starch chinos. When it comes to training, my single goal is to check off every scheduled workout on the calendar. If the schedule calls for five workouts in a week, then I'm going to do those five workouts, even if it feels like my ankles have been through a rock crusher. I could care less about quality workouts or ultimate results. I just want to hold up my plan at the end of the training cycle—like Newt Gingrich with his hole-puncher in one hand and Contract with America in the other—and have it covered in red—always red—X marks.

Another thing: if the schedule calls for a long run today, then it must be done today. Not tomorrow. Not the day after tomorrow. Not even if the weather is like The Day After Tomorrow. So, when the schedule recently called for a Saturday-morning twelve miler and there was no baby-sitter to be found, it was damn the wind chill, full speed ahead with the stroller. When I got it, it seemed like something I had to have. Moreover, I knew it was good for me. But then, over time, the novelty wore off. But you feel guilty and so you force yourself to use it, but it's no longer fun, it's a burden. Finally, you abandon any pretense of enjoyment and stick it in a corner with the BowFlex, Showtime Rotisserie, and complete works of Henry James. I speak, of course, about Junior. Not the jogging stroller, I love that thing. With its cotton-light frame, Bontrager wheels, and pimp-my-stroller paint job, the machine is flat-out cool. Even Lance Armstrong would look good resting in its saddle, "Live Strong" rattle in one hand, Sheryl Crow action figure in the other (the one where you pull the string in her back and she sings, "All I wanna do is have some fun with your ex-husband").

So off we went. A mile or so into the run, I didn't think there'd be any problems. Besides, we've done this before and Junior is so cute when he thaws out, the way he changes colors like a mood ring. Junior hadn't mustered much resistance when I moved him from his bed to the stroller. But then he wriggled out of his blankie. I had fastened it snugger than a straitjacket—for thermal purposes, of course—but he is dogged, the little Houdini. By the second mile, his efforts at unraveling the blankie had generated enough body heat to thaw his facial muscles, and he began to, how should I put it—vocalize his displeasure. The tone was somewhere between car alarm and seventh-grade cheerleading squad that just ran into Clay Aiken at The Cheesecake Factory. He held that note longer than Gilda in Rigoletto. But I read that you're supposed to run through pain, and I assume that includes the aural variety, and so I pressed on.

By the third mile, the little sport looked like a member of the Shackleton expedition. His lips had an Aqua Velva tint and his little runny nose had frozen into two snotsicles. Adorable. He implored me to take him back home, which I agreed to do. I soothed him by saying, "Only ten more miles, Junior." His generation is so impatient. Unable to wait, he invoked the "sippie cup" gambit. As we tore down the hill, I in full stride, he swiftly lodged his sippie cup in the spokes. It's a little known fact that a similar incident in the Paris-Roubaix Classic led to the early retirement of Bernard Hinault.

His toddler treachery complete, the immutable laws of physics took over. The stroller stopped. I didn't. And that brings us full circle, to that silhouetted figure gliding over the stroller. Junior and I made eye contact as my trajectory went, far too quickly in my opinion, from horizontal to scud missile. I think he winked at me, but since the incident, my memory often fails me. A mind is as terrible a thing to ricochet off asphalt. I remember regaining consciousness and seeing a cluster of walkers elbow-swinging their way towards me. "God bless you, walkers," I kept muttering to myself, even as the first stepped on my face and headed straight for my male heir. Junior had already fished my cell phone out the back of the stroller and called a cab—an impressive feat in this town—and his cherubic face betrayed no hint of his patricidal conduct.

The sippie cup, I knew, would be the evidence I needed to put him away for a long time, but the power walkers, after seeing

Junior home, returned to stomp me into what I'm sure they hoped would be the Big Sleep. One even removed Junior's snotsicles and tried to booger-shiv me between the ribs. When I regained consciousness the second time, the sippie cup was nowhere to be found, and those geese had a shifty look about them. I got myself to all fours and then to my feet. I made a tourniquet using my outer layer and started hobbling, not towards home but rather down the trail. The schedule, after all, called for ten more miles.

We have a second recommendation and that is to purchase this product:

MUSHER PERFORMANCE JOGGING STROLLER. You'll enjoy hours of strolling with your kids with this high-performance jogging stroller designed for maximum comfort and an ultra-smooth ride. The super-light aluminum frame provides superior shock absorbency and complete support for the Barcalounger-style seat. The Bose audio system is compatible with Sirius or XM Radio. Children are harnessed to the front with a series of padded leather gang lines and tug lines. This is the perfect stroller for the avid runner ready to "turn the tables on these freeloaders in my house." Available in Only Child or Brood models. $389.99.

Embracing the Elements
We don't mind if you train in all the elements, but we encourage you to become a Goldilocks racer—only race if the weather is "just right." We could explain how heat, cold, and wind can affect the body, but these stories from some of our running readers are a more vivid illustration.

Heat—The Fire This Time

Dear Secret Book of Running:

I survived the 2007 Chicago Marathon, also known as The Great Chicago Fire Part II, and this is my story. Before I begin, I can see you staring at me, so let me explain why I look like an over-cooked then freeze-dried rotisserie chicken. Yesterday, I crawled out of an ice freezer in front of a convenience store in the Chicago Loop. It's where I headed soon after crossing the finish line. It seemed like the fastest way to reduce my core temperature, which I have on good information that, had it increased three additional degrees, would have qualified me for star status at NASA. One day later, after lying there like the least flattering piece of red snapper at the local fishmonger, and after telling several startled customers to "Get your ice and shut the door!" I am here to offer a cautionary tale for those runners attempting a marathon on a day when the forecast reads like a Ray Bradbury novel—Fahrenheit 451. For as I reflect on the day's events, there were several warning signs that, had I heeded them, might have saved me from my destiny: Toast. Burnt Toast. Both sides, no marmalade.

Before a race in those conditions—here, the narrator whispers in voice-over: "We've secretly replaced the South Side with Death Valley. Let's see if the marathoners notice"—you ask yourself questions like "Should I change my pacing strategy?" and "How many more clothes can I take off without getting arrested?" and "Has Bain de Soleil always been a name sponsor?" The starting corral of a major marathon is always a bit of a mosh pit, so you will forgive me if I misheard the announcements from the race director. From my position, I am positive he said, "Welcome to the Cairo Marathon!" and then, after the puzzled roar fizzed out like shook cola, "Congratulations on being part of the world's largest schvitz!"

Before I could say, "Did he say Schlitz?" the starting gun popped. Once, twice, then three times. I learned later that was the heat causing several transformers to explode. But it was signal enough, and we were on our way. Over the PA system, someone sang a remake of the Rocky Theme. Was it just me, or did the singer say, "Gonna Fry Now!" I can't be sure either way.

We were only a mile down the road when the great benevolent deity in the sky began to train its magnifying glass on the runners. Like squirming insects or uncredited extras in War of the Worlds, runners began to incinerate all around me, their charred singlets littering LaSalle Street. I took evasive action, using serpentine movements to avoid their fate. As the concrete sizzled and the air steamed, I felt like a dress oxford at the dry cleaners where the owner had expressly requested extra steam! I had not sweated that much since my last IRS audit. Someone handed me a cup of Tabasco.

A few miles later, we were near Lincoln Park and a slight breeze blew towards us. I turned to the runner to my right: "It smells like seafood, don't you think?" The runner just stared at me with a look that said: "I'm not being impolite. I would respond to you, but my lips have melted off." But a runner to my left butted in: "It's Lake Michigan! Lake Michigan is boiling!" Don't be ridiculous!" a race volunteer chimed in. "It's only a simmer." Another volunteer proffered: "Crab claw?"

Reassured, we pressed on, even though I felt like Nicolas Cage at the end of The Wicker Man. We passed a small memorial service for the last surviving ice cube in Cook County. I heard an announcement over the PA system that the first runner had just crossed the finish line. It was Mr. Heatmiser.

By the time we hit Old Town, the race really started to get strange. As we approached an aid station with a Hawaiian Luau *theme, I noticed that they had laid hot coals along one lane of the road. The remaining runners were all heading for the coals— because they were cooler than the road. Did I mention that all our shoes had melted long before Wrigleyville? I was kicking myself for not buying Mizuno's flame-retardant flats. For some runners, the scorching heat began to penetrate their skulls and singe their brains. At the luau, one runner leaped onto a spit-roasting pig, clinging impressively for three revolutions. A short piece down the road, another runner headed into a coffee shop yelling, "Fight fire with fire!" He came running out with a Grande House Blend and poured it over his head. From my vantage, it did not look iced; no trace of whip cream could be seen. A Barista and a medic took him away.*

By the halfway point, I felt like a campfire marshmallow over a campfire in the hands of the kid who liked his black. All around me, runners were melting like the Germans who kept their eyes open at the end of Raiders of the Lost Ark. *I paused at a gel station, but the only choices were flame-broiled or pan-seared. The adjacent water stop was serving Flaming Dr. PowerAde Shots. A few blocks later, in the Pilsen neighborhood, gentle women cooked huevos rancheros on the sidewalk. "You need the protein, muchacho!" cautioned a worried spectator. Still I ran, passing Al Gore, of all people, in Bronzeville, who shrugged his shoulders and said, "I'm not saying. I'm just saying."*

At Mile 17, I fell into a burning ring of fire. I think it had been created by the strafing runs from the helicopters with the flame-throwers mounted to their bellies. Still, I ran. My pace slowed considerably at Mile 19 because the asphalt bubbled and gurgled and had a Le Brea Tar Pit consistency. I pressed on, even as the lava started to flow down Michigan Avenue. By that point, the aid stations were out of water. But helpful fire-eaters from the circus offered to jab their torches down our throats. "It will cauterize your thirst buds!" promised a Fellini-esque character with dubious medical credentials. I tried to distract myself through mental disassociation. I am not a runner. I am an orange rolling down the street. No, an apple. No a banana. A banana being flamed tableside for bananas foster.

Despite all that, I kept moving forward, passing 21, 22, 23, 24, and 25 in a blaze. And when I say no pun intended, I mean no pun intended. It was so hard to stay upright and propel myself forward when my natural instinct, ingrained since elementary school, was to stop, drop, and roll. In the last mile, I ran like a man with his hair on fire. Because. My. Hair. Was. On. Fire. I made it to the brown, scarred, smoldering, post-apocalyptic desert-scape that was once Grant Park. Buckingham Fountain spewed fireballs in every direction. Crossing the finish line, the clock hung limply like something out of a Dali painting. To my right, I saw about a dozen cups of cool water resting on a table. I went to grab one, but was stopped by a volunteer. 'Don't!" she screamed. "They're filled with runners!" Sure enough, there was the diminutive elite field, floating on their backs in the paper cups, trying to cool off like the rest of us. The finisher's medals had been replaced by cremation urns.

And that is exactly how it happened at the 2007 Chicago Marathon, the year I paid for Chicago and got creme brulee'd for free.

Cold—The Iceman Cometh, But the Race Director Leaveth

And if you think heat can wreak havoc on race day, consider the dangers of cold weather. You are just asking for it if you run a race with frosty, frostbite, frozen, or arctic in the name. If you truly must get your core temperature in the teens, we recommend the professional ice-fishing circuit or a visit to our grandmother's condominium in Florida.

Dear Secret Book of Running:

I suppose I was asking for it when I registered for a race billed as the "Frostbite Half-Marathon." You should never enter a race with a dubious adjective like that. I thought I had learned my lesson at the Vampire Bats 15K. When I left my house on Saturday at 8:30 for the 11:00 am start, the temperature was in the mid-20s and dropping. There was an inch or more of snow from the night before, and the putty-gray sky was spraying a Whitman's Sampler of snow, ice, sleet, and rain. My decision to attempt to drive to the start area and actually run the race was the most ill-advised cold weather decision since Ernest Shackleton decided to see March of the Penguins live.

On this race day, the primary challenge was not getting to the finish line. Rather, it was getting to the start line. The drive to the park is usually forty-five minutes from our house. But with the slick roads, I gave myself what I thought was plenty of time to grandpa it in the right lane. I did not count on the jackknifed eighteen-wheeler that shut down I-40, causing a standstill on the Interstate for most of Weekend Edition and all of Car Talk. By the time I reached the Park entrance and slid into the parking lot, it was ten minutes to start time. I had enough time to pin my number and ditch my sweats, and then the race was on. So much for warming up or weighing whether to wear trainers or snowshoes.

The steep hills of the Frostbite course would have been challenging under even the best of circumstances. But today, with the aforementioned arctic precipitation (what the meterologists called a "wintry mix") and roads glazed with ice, snow, and slush,

it was sheer folly. You may think I'm exaggerating, but some runners had their own Sherpas. Others had family dogs they could
eat if things got really tough along the way. The race director,
instead of firing a starter's pistol, yelled, "Mush!"

The first mile was an education in friction. It quickly became
apparent that, if I was going to stay upright, I had to run where
it crunched. Otherwise, the course was an icy place where my
feet could find no purchase. Or like Mick Jagger said, "I can't get
no satis-traction." There were some parts of the course with a
relatively clear path through the ice, but invariably it veered away
from the shortest route.

I climbed and descended for six miles without incident until a
volunteer waved three of us down the wrong fork in the road. We
were about twenty seconds down this road less traveled before
another volunteer shouted at us to turn around. I was upset, but
not as much as another group of runners who were also led
astray. They ran for miles, got stuck in the cold, and ended up re-
creating "the huddle" described in <u>Into Thin Air</u>.

Would you believe that despite the temperature, the lack of
a warm-up, the road conditions, and pulling a "method air" on
the final hill and barely landing it, I still nailed a PR? It is amaz-
ing how the lure of hot chocolate, or the fear of looking like Jack
Nicholson at the end of The Shining, will make you run faster
than you thought possible.

Wind—We Can't Seem to Forget It, Its Wind Song Stays on Our Mind

Not to be outdone, wind can be just as debilitating as
heat and cold. Only the wind can induce that cartoon-char-
acter feeling of spinning your legs furiously while gaining no
ground. We have encountered wind in many races, and it was

never beneath our wings. Like a guest on the *Jerry Springer Show*, wind always finds a way to get up in your face and stay there. Tail winds exist in theory, like a balanced budget or Sasquatch, but we have yet to encounter one. We don't have a specific example or racing in a headwind, but let's just say that it has happened on many occasions and it wasn't a breeze. We suggest you avoid any race in the Midwest or along the coasts, where the wind can be fierce and a race billed as a scenic run along the beach can turn into "Adventures in Sandblasting." But the South has its share of wicked winds, too, and let's not forget the Hudson Hawk and other prevailing gales of the Eastern Corridor. Come to think, we have also seen meteorological warnings that it is "blowing like a mother!" in the West and American Southwest. Sorry, but we're getting winded just trying to think of a location where you will be safe from wind.

Rain, Hail, Sleet, Lightning, and Frogs

Those are bad, too. Best to skip the race and sue for a refund of your registration fee.

Making Excuses

They descend on the finish line of every race like locusts in the Old Testament. They are as certain as an ill-fitting Speedo on a Memorial Day beach. I'm talking about excuses. We hear them. We make them. And frankly, they're getting a little old, a little cliché. Nothing against clichés, although we personally avoid them like the plague. And nothing against excuses—we founded and built this country on excuses. But nobody wants to hear for the hundredth time how the dog ate your running partner, you were pacing the walkers, or you would have run faster if all your finisher medals didn't weigh you down. What, you don't wear all your medals to your races? Perhaps you're reading the wrong book. As excuses go, we think we can do better. Here are some proposals:

Old Excuse: *"It was too cold/hot."*
New Excuse: *"Climate change!" or "Global warming!"*

We call this the Goldilocks excuse. Are we talking about weather or porridge? The temperature is never just right. But a better excuse acknowledges the larger forces at work. Scientists say climate change is causing a rise in sea levels, thawing of the Greenland ice sheet, stronger hurricanes, hotter summers, acidification of the oceans, and a flurry of change-of-address cards among islanders in Papua New Guinea. What scientists won't tell you, but we will, is that climate change also explains why you were vomiting on the roadside with a mile to go. It's called The Butterfly Effect. Incidentally, here is something we have always wondered about: If a butterfly can flap its wings on one side of the globe and cause a tsunami on the other, why don't we just kill all those murderous insects? Regardless, "climate change" is an excellent excuse and will make you sound scientific and up-to-date. We like to finish it with, "If the current administration had signed the Kyoto Protocols, I would have owned that course."

Old Excuse: *"I went out too fast/slow."*
New Excuse: *"My parents didn't love me."*

This is another of the Goldilocks variations. Of course you went out too fast or too slow. Who goes out just right?

Even and negative splits are the Bigfoot and Loch Ness Monster of road racing. We all want to believe they exist, but—ask yourself—have you ever seen them? Dredging up your childhood traumas is a much better alternative. They make other people uncomfortable and less likely to challenge your excuse. Your father ignored you, your mother was cold and distant, and they locked you in your room and fed you sweet and savory crepes until you graduated high school. "The better to slide under your door, my dear." To this day, if we see Crepes Suzette on a menu, we break out into a rash. If your father's swearing to a grocery clerk that he could in fact "redeem" you along with empty glass bottles for fifteen cents doesn't explain your 10K time, then we don't know what will.

Old Excuse: *"The course was hilly."*
New Excuse: *"The course was haunted."*

This one requires eye contact. You really have to sell the line. It helps if you cross the finish a little ashen-faced, never a problem for us. Our staff's pallor has prompted our fans to refer to us as "pasty but tasty."

Old Excuse: *"I didn't eat properly."*
New Excuse: *"I had one too many of the Clams Casino last night."*

You say your diet isn't what it should be. Join the club. If you're going to use a food or drink excuse, you need to individualize it, give it some snap and distinction. We like the "Clams Casino" excuse because we are confident that a dish involving clams, butter, shallots, and bacon won't be on the pre-race pasta party menu. A nice addition is "I knew I shouldn't have had those oysters at mile 8."

Old Excuse: *"Just didn't feel right out there."*
New Excuse: "[Insert name of politician here] "

We are loath to sully the Norman Rockwell wholesomeness of this book and the great sport of running by mentioning politics, our great American side stitch, but indulge me for a moment as we hearken back to a simpler time, before 9/11, the Iraq War, and *American Idol*. Was society as coarse back then? That was the Clinton Administration, so yes I suppose it was. Let's go further back, before cilantro. No, that won't work either. The point is that the problems in this country, starting with your race performance, are the fault of the president or Congress. Is it the majority or the minority party? Yes.

Old Excuse: *"Forgot to start my watch."*
New Excuse: *"Battery died on my heart-rate monitor…and my pacemaker."*

We offer this excuse in the spirit of inclusion. It may not work for everyone, but at most of our races we get lapped by what appears to be a casting call for *Cocoon*. We read these stories about men and women in their sixties, seventies, or older remaining active, and we see with our own eyes what these grandmasters can do at local races, and it fills me with hope—hope that the race start will conflict with the early-bird dinner at K&W Cafeteria. Come on, old-timers, you had your shot. This is our time to shine.

Old Excuse: *"The course was long."*
New Excuse: *"My lawyer screwed me."*

We will complain about the course being short because we want our money's worth. But we find ourselves in the minority on that one. As for the new excuse, it's no secret that we're a litigious society. We are looking to our lawyer for advice on everything from the minimum standard of care required to avoid having the state take our son to the appropriate portion of peanut butter to smear on our bagel. So when things don't turn out right at the local 8K, despite the hefty retainer we've forked over, we're looking to inflict "serious personal injury" on that Brooks Brothers–wearing no-account barrister.

Old Excuse: *"I wasn't trying for a PR."*
New Excuse: *"Somebody said PR, so I stopped to call my agent."*

People talk about PRs or PR all the time, and I say if you want good PR, get yourself a decent agent, start reading *Daily Variety*, and please do something with that hair. I mean, there's a reason why they murdered Caesar—it was because of the haircut.

Old Excuse: *"I waited too long to take fluids and became dehydrated."*
New Excuse: *"I refused to take the fluids. Haven't you heard of fluoridation?"*

People don't want to admit it, but it's true—the race volunteers are trying to poison you. I can no longer sit back and allow this Communist infiltration, Communist indoctrination, Communist subversion, and the international Communist conspiracy to sap and impurify all of our precious bodily fluids. We know what they are serving at those aid stations and it has to stop. If you don't believe me, just ask Mulder and Scully. I am all for complete effort at my races, but not at the expense of the purity and essence of my natural bodily fluids.

Old Excuse: *"The lead bike led me astray."*

We don't have a new excuse for this one because it only applies to the elite runners, and frankly, their excuses arouse no sympathy in our breast. Well, perhaps a sweat bead worth of sympathy. For we once found ourselves right behind the pace bike. It was a dune buggy to be exact, and as we ran behind it, it started to swerve left and right. Perhaps this was how they wheeled the course, we thought, and continued to follow it, even as it started doing figure eights and wheelies. The crowd loved it, but it infuriated us. If we could have caught it, we would have made it eat his fez, tassel and all. We learned later that it was a parade, not a race. Damn Shriners. We take no blame for the error. When we are up front, we don't look back, so we never noticed that the pack had matching uniforms and musical instruments.

If you can recall a few of these excuses, then whatever happens at your next race, it won't be your fault.

/ / /

Let's Go Race: Racing and Race Strategy

Learn From Your Mistakes

You can learn something from every race you run. You should take some time to assess every race performance and compile a list of factors that affected your day. We heard from one marathon runner whose story resonated with us. He missed qualifying for Boston by less than thirty seconds, or roughly one second per mile. This is what he learned:

Dear Secret Book of Running:

When you come so close to your goal—I'm talking "Rocky" close, I'm talking photo finish close (if you have a half-minute shutter speed exposure on your camera)—you can't help but look back and think about the things you could have done differently. A couple of small decisions here and there could have made the Boston-qualifying difference. You can't get in the DeLorean and change the result, but you can learn from your choices so you'll know better next time.

With that in mind, here are some of the things I did during the SunTrust National Marathon in Washington, DC, that probably cost me a few seconds here and there and that I promise myself I won't do in my next marathon:

- *Will not argue with the bag drop guy about why he can't check my bag to my final destination.*
- *Will not stop for bipartisan prayer breakfast on Capitol Hill.*
- *Will not rescue cat (Is that you, Socks?) from tree.*
- *Will not accept Cabinet position and submit to vetting process and confirmation hearing.*
- *Will not peel off from course for "half-smoke" at Ben's Chili Bowl.*
- *Will not help Helen Thomas cross the street.*
- *Will not resign Cabinet post, accept job on K Street, and lobby former colleagues.*
- *Will not form political action committee for hip-hop causes—TUPAC.*
- *Will not leave town to for town hall meeting with constituents back in the district.*
- *Will not recite "I Have a Marathon Dream" from Lincoln Memorial.*

What I will do, I hope, is run 27 seconds faster. And if I don't, I won't point to the female runner ahead of me and say, Marion Barry-style, "The b$%#! set me up!" Looking back, that was completely inappropriate.

Every Race Is an Experiment

You may have heard the phrase "every race is an experiment." Every race is an opportunity to try different tactics, different methods, to find out what triggers your best performance. It could be a longer warm-up or a shorter warm-up. It could be a few extra strides or some dynamic stretching. It might be a first mile run ten, twenty, or forty-five seconds slower than goal pace. You might try eating during the race. Or not eating. It could be a different pair of shoes. It might be a combination of all these things. You will run a host of races over your career, so why not try to figure out your optimal race preparation and strategy.

But you will not do this because you are a runner. You are not Jonas Salk. You are not Niels Bohr. You do not experiment. You do not adhere to the Scientific Method, only the JAR Method. You care only for pacing tables, not the Periodic Table of Elements. Nature may abhor a vacuum, but you embrace a rut. You are going to do it the way you did it the first time you ran a race and you will repeat it until you can race no longer. Let the PhD students experiment. When it comes to racing, whether it works or not, you would rather be a running recidivist, a repeat offender.

Race Strategy

Many factors go into race strategy. Here are a few pointers to help you have a successful race:

- **Shock and aw**. Coaches will recommend that you start slowly, but we suggest you shock the competition by flying off the starting line and winning the first fifty meters. Then pull up lame because you pulled a hamstring and listen to the competition say, "Aw, that's too bad. He might have won the race had he not injured himself."
- **Pick an off-brand distance**. We recommend that you avoid marathons or 5Ks. Most people seem to know what a respectable time is on those races. But if you run an 8K, 15K, or 30K, your average Joe can't do the math to figure out if you won the whole damn thing or finished a day later.

- **Dream weaver.** The shortest distance between two points is a straight line, but if there's thirty thousand runners between those points, get ready to do some weaving and zigzagging. In a marathon, you may end up running an extra mile, and it is perfectly acceptable to deduct fifteen minutes per mile from your official chip time.

- **Make sure everything you wear is new.** Why go into a race with a tried and true outfit? Instead, why not start fresh with new shoes, shorts, socks, and shirt? If you develop a blister or suffer race-ending chafing, it can only be because your gear was not new enough. Also, leave the tags on so that if you don't run fast (translation: the new gear does not work), you can wring it out and return it for a refund.

- **Own the water stations.** Keep yourself well hydrated by visiting the water stations early and often. Do not be afraid to drink several cups at each station, to pour the Gatorade tub over your head like you just won the Super Bowl, or to floss and rinse.

- **Communicate, as necessary, with faster runners.** It is inevitable that other runners will pass you during the race. You should not trip them. But there is no harm in cursing them, either loudly or under your breath. That is, after all, what the JAR Method is all about.

- **Gamble with caution.** If you are going to wager with someone over who will win, your best chances are to seek out someone either wearing the race shirt or wearing cutoff blue jeans. This will not guarantee a payoff, but it does improve your chances.

- **Know your cutoff time and hold something in reserve**. Most big races have a "sweeper" at the end of the race. It might be a group of walkers, some bicyclists, or a street-sweeping truck followed by a steamroller. In those instances where it is the latter, you will want to have some reserve energy in the tank. If not, the phrase "I was totally flat for that race" could take on a whole new meaning.

Post-Race Recovery

A proper race-recovery plan is as important as a proper training plan. *The Secret Book of Running* would never abandon you at the finish line. No, we want you to recover for the next race—which might be the next day or that afternoon. So here are some tips to transition from once race to the next:

First, don't collapse after you cross the finish line. That serves no purpose because the race is over. If you're going to collapse, you want to do it long before you get to the finish line. We recommend the first mile of the race. That gives you a greater range of legitimate finish times that you "would have run" but for the collapse. Be sure to memorize and rehearse your "collapse excuse" as part of your pre-race taper.

When you cross the finish line, stay on your feet and keep walking. If it's a race without chip timing, use this time to muscle your way past smaller or less-experienced runners in the finish chute. You just might improve your finishing time that way. Keep moving all the way to where they post the results. Stand there and immediately start complaining loudly about why all the results haven't been posted. (Caveat: if twelve pages of single-spaced, eight-point font results are posted already, say nothing.)

After you see your results in print and protest vociferously that the course was long and the clock was fast, do some grazing. Fruit salad is an excellent high-vitamin, low-calorie snack. Use this opportunity to snag enough bananas, oranges, and apples to make a fruit salad that will last for a week or more. Your schwag bag makes for an excellent receptacle to carry everything back to your car.

Some races offer runners a free massage. Investigate this beforehand and, if there will be a masseuse on the premises, plan accordingly. We recommend you bring, in addition to your racing flats and BodyGlide, a facial and back-waxing kit along with spa robe and slippers. When your massage is complete, insist that your masseuse give you a facial and waxing. After all, you probably paid fifteen dollars for this race, and you are looking past the frustrating lack of a Jacuzzi and cucumber slices in the water.

Don't forget to stretch—the truth about your race performance. You may be fatigued after the stress of the race. That is normal. But as soon as possible, you want to remember what got you to this point—the JAR Method. And it is likely that there are one or more runners you have good reason to be jealous of, feel anger towards, and resent. Picture them in your mind's eye or, if they are still milling around (in their Boston Marathon windbreakers, no doubt), glare at them. It's time to start training again.

Dress Like a Champion Today:
Tips for Racing Attire

"Look the part, be the part!" Prop Joe said that on *The Wire*, and like everything else ever said on that show—"It is what it is." "A man must have a code." "Yo, they got any Honey Nut up in here?"—it is the absolute gospel truth.

So let's talk about race-day attire. You have to look the part. You want to dress like you're a member of the Olympic team to give yourself the mental boost to run fast. You need to wear a singlet—that top that they used to call a muscle shirt. No T-shirts, no long-sleeve shirts, technical or otherwise, no compression tops, no running jackets, no mesh half-shirts like the one Scott Glenn wore in *Urban Cowboy*. Look, we've tried them all and they don't work. You want a free-flowing singlet. We usually go with white because it matches our legs. Please do not wear the race shirt to race. If you see someone wearing the race shirt (him over there in the cut-off jeans), that's the guy you want to bet you can beat.

And would it be too much to ask to tuck it in? Not only is it more aerodynamic, it looks nicer. We know everyone wants to expose their shirttails these days, and we are not here to cast judgment on that sort of trendy fashion abomination except to say that you probably also think it's cool to wear flip-flops on an airplane and we bet you wore a purple shirt and tie to the office back when Regis Philbin did it on *Who Wants to be a Millionaire*. Whatever you do before the race is your business, but come race morning, tuck in your singlet. When you cross the finish line, you can pull it out with a flourish like Prince Fielder when he hits a walk-off home run.

We put the girls in a trance when we're wearing track pants, but on race day we wear traditional running shorts. You might also know them as short-shorts or hot pants. Now is the time to show some leg. Forget the tights or half-tights. Don't show up in culottes or down-to-the-knee retro Washington Bullets gym shorts. We don't care if your dribble penetration and stop-and-pop are lethal. This isn't Rucker Park. It's a marathon. Slip on the embarrassingly short shorts, preferably with the split down the side, and even better if it has piping to match your singlet.

As for shoes, we get this question a lot and so we will answer it now. With all-white running shoes, the traditional rule is that you can wear them from Memorial Day to Labor Day. But if you're in the Deep South, it is acceptable to wear them from Easter forward, so long as it is warm outside. Moving on.

If it's cold, there is nothing wrong with gloves and arm-sleeves. If at all possible they should match. We know that when our CEO wears the sleeves it can be a disappointment for the ladies, and some men, who bought tickets to see the gun show. If you're going to do the combination, we recommend black because it evokes Audrey Hepburn in *Breakfast at Tiffany's*.

And that's about it. Leave all that stuff you used in training behind. No Fuel Belts, none of those backpack contraptions that look like undeployed parachutes, no twin bandoleers of fluids and gel. Stuff the gels in your pocket and drink the fluids on the course.

Do we need to mention the fanny pack? The smartphone? The race belt? Two watches? Pinning things to your shirt? Are you a marathoner or a float? If you feel like you need a visor, it's probably going to be too warm and you shouldn't be racing. And please save the Stormtrooper carrying the blaster outfit for Halloween.

The one accessory that we will endorse is a pair of calf guards. They have a pedigree: Paula Radcliffe wore a pair when she set the women's world record. They are supposed to assist with blood flow and reduce muscle fatigue. We like the way they feel and the way they warm our calves in 35-degree weather. And you can't argue with results or the implicit homage to Michael Cooper.

So look the part and be the part, marathoners. And if you do, in your next race you may not come up as short as your race bottoms.

To Jam or Not to Jam

Should you or should you not run with an MP3 player? We, along with most race directors, say no. We embrace the Zen-like moments the unbudded runner gets from hearing honking horns, yelling drivers, and taunting kids on school buses during one's daily route. Many race directors strictly prohibit MP3 players on the course, so they can ensure that you will hear some moron shout that "you're almost done" when you're less than one-third into the race. In these races, the runner has no choice but to follow the rules and leave Lady Gaga in the "Check Baggage" tent.

But we do not dismiss the powerful testimonies we get from some runners who insist on the "boogie boost" they get from their MP3 player. Consider this letter, for example, and make your own decision on whether you want to be wired wire-to-wire at your next race:

As a marathon runner, I define myself by what I am not. When I read articles about these elite runners, they always seem to expound on how they are in tune with every muscle in their body, how no twitch goes unnoticed. These runners anticipate and welcome the pain that comes with racing. They even have a name for it: association. Well, I am not a dues-paying member of that association. More effete than elite, during the second half of any marathon I'm grasping for every distraction I can find to take my mind off the bear traps clamping down on my legs. For years, I tried talking myself through the pain, but my brain usually dismissed my feeble pleas quicker than Donald Trump in the boardroom. Nowadays, however, with iPods as ubiquitous as mullets at a NASCAR race, music has become my best option for race disassociation. It has been my experience that a judiciously crafted play list—what I call my "racetrack"—is a powerful panacea for those times in the marathon when, to paraphrase Christina Aguilera, "my heart is saying let's go, but my body's saying no."

Note the use of the word *judicious.* A racetrack is a tricky beast. It can put you on its back and potato-sack-carry you through the last 5K, but it can also sink you quicker than the *Lusitania.* The key to any racetrack is timing. When the starting gun sounds at your next marathon, the last thing you want to hear is Survivor's "Eye of the Tiger." Sure, Paul Tergat may be sucking off your tailpipe for the first eight hundred meters, but you'll be toast before you see the first mile marker. From then on, you'll feel like you have one a funny car parachute on your back, and not even *Jock Jams II* will be able to save you.

No, for the marathon distance, you need to ease into it. You probably shouldn't even turn your music player on for the first thirty minutes. But if you must, we recommend Hemingway. Ernest Hemingway. We know one runner who found that those clipped, staccato sentences work well with his cadence. He says you should stick to *The Sun Also Rises* and stay away from the bullfighting and marlin fishing. Mississippi runners may also want to try William Faulkner. He was Southern and did say, in a different context, that he believed that man would not merely endure, he would prevail. And that, after all, is what all marathoners want. Faulkner has been a steady running companion for me. I'll never forget the look on that perky sorority girl's face when we were treadmill running side by side, and my head was gyrating like a bobble doll, and she asked what I was listening to, and I said: "Absalom, Absalom!" I enjoy Faulkner's run-on sentences so much that I have created a track session using his Nobel Prize acceptance speech. I call the workout my Yoknapataw-pha 800s. (That line killed at the Ole Miss English Department Faculty Picnic.) Our one caution with Faulkner is that you may want to avoid *As I Lay Dying*. Positive thoughts only, please.

Once you make it past the first 10K of the marathon, it's time for the real music. Here, you need to find what works best for you. It might be rap, gospel, country, alternative, classical, pop, polka, or some combination thereof. (Go ahead and insert your John Tesh joke of choice here.) If ELO is your EPO, then go with it. Personally, my marathon cocktail contains a little pop, a little rap, some classic rock, a healthy dose of movie themes, and, for the twist, a show tune or two. [Note to self: download "What a Feeling" from *Flashdance*.]

I stick with movie themes, or songs from TV and movie soundtracks, for two reasons. First, I don't come from a music background and so I am oblivious to most recorded music. Growing up, after dinner we sat around while my father played the lawnmower. My church forbade music, snapping, tapping, and humming, insisting that only digestive and guttural sounds would get the congregation to heaven. So, unless a song is played in a movie or on TV, it may be as catchy as *The Magic Flute*, but I probably won't hear it. Second, I like these songs because they allow for double disassociation. I need more than mere disassociation. And with songs from movies, I get the music, and the film associated with the music, to take my mind off my lung-searing suffering. I have found that you should not underestimate the power of the racetrack: Pick the right tunes and you could PR in wet cement.

I'll give you an example: I always strategically place the theme from *Superman* on my racetrack. It's a soaring score that immediately gets my heart thumping faster. I often run the duration of this song with right arm extended, fist clenched, chin tucked into sternum, and left arm triangulated with hand clasping waist. You should try it sometime, particularly if you're out doing a long training run alone. When I hear it, I rarely think of Superman. Rather, I think of Jerry Seinfeld and the "I Choose Not to Run!" episode, because this song was playing when Jerry jumped the gun and won the race. Even in that above-mentioned posture, I can usually take thirty seconds off my mile split with no perceived additional effort.

I always place "Superman" past the two-hour mark, where he'll be needed most. I will usually start my racetrack—after the literature lecture or fireside chat—with the theme from *Chariots of Fire*, a standard that belongs on every racetrack just like "My Way" belongs in every lounge in Las Vegas. Then I might toss in some Coldplay or U2 or vintage Beastie Boys, anything to pass the time. I backload my racetrack for the second half of the marathon, saving my greatest hits for the last hour. I always include The Who's "Baba O'Riley." For some reason, I like Bowie as well. For the beginning of a marathon, I might pluck some of the Portuguese covers from *The Life Aquatic*, but in the last hour, I turn to "Under Pressure" and "Young Americans." "Under Pressure" reminds me of the opening scene in *The Girl Next Door*, a movie that was funnier than it had any right to be. And "Young Americans" just has a peppy introduction. A recent addition is Jamiroquai's "Canned Heat," the tune that had Napoleon Dynamite dancing for Pedro. I don't think that needs any further explanation. You know this boogie is for real.

As I approach the last 10K of the marathon, I lean heavily on the movie themes: *Last of the Mohicans, Glory, Star Wars, Driving Miss Daisy*. I have always wanted to time my finish to coincide with *Raiders of the Lost Ark*, so when I entered the chute, I could tell a volunteer, "You throw me the medal. I throw you the chip." But just as you should always begin with *Chariots of Fire*, you should always finish with *Rocky*. I know it's cliché, but clichés are cliché for a reason. It's because they're, well, cliché. Nothing gives you more bang per decibel than the Rocky Suite, in all its funky seventies glory. How many times have I stumbled across the finish line and collapsed into the arms of a volunteer, muttering, "There ain't gonna be no rematch?" Too many to count.

So, if you're running sub-2:10 and you monitor your body signals like a seismologist in San Francisco, then you can disregard our advice. But if you're like so many others who read this book and then went on to trounce their competition, we urge you to re-jigger your brain in your next marathon by using your taper to fine-tune your racetrack. As the Sugarhill Gang once urged: "Tonto, jump on it, jump on it, jump on it!"

When to Race—Schedule
the Madness for March

Now that you know how to train for a race, the question becomes: when should you race? For the shorter distances, anything from 5K to half-marathon, you can race them just about year round, although any race in the middle of summer will be miserable. With the marathon, however, some months are definitely better than others. We believe there is no better month than March to run a Boston-qualifying time. April, the Boston month, is too fraught with the vagaries of weather conditions. You might have a cold day, but you might also get a muggy, warm spring morning. Unless you're willing to travel to the most northern American climes, May is out of the question for the same reasons. We don't think we have to say anything about June through September. There may be some fun races in there, and some interesting locations, and some opportunities for epic adventures, but there's nothing happening in those months that will put you in the best position to qualify for Boston.

October has some of the great marathons in America— Twin Cities and Chicago. The problem is that to train for them, you have to do the core of your training in August and September. This is far from ideal if you live in the South. But if you can put in some solid training in the heat, you are usually, though not always, rewarded with a cold race day, which makes you feel like someone strapped a rocket to your back.

November is probably better than October, since you get the cooler fall temps for your hardest pre-race workouts. December is probably better still, for similar reasons, though you have to work around Thanksgiving, which can be a problem if you're a pie-baking zealot. The problem with

November or December marathons is that they are in the late fall, and the fall is one of the peak racing seasons, and in most places, you will have a rash of races that tempt you every weekend. A race here or there as part of your marathon training is encouraged, but too much racing is not a good idea. Let's face it, the marathon is a jealous mistress, and more often than not your weekend should be given over to long runs, not trying to PR in the local 5K. If you can ignore those races, then a November or December race is close to ideal, but if you're one of these weak-minded runners who takes his or her eye off the ball in pursuit of local Grand Prix age-group glory, you might want to avoid scheduling your marathon during the holiday season.

January and February are good marathon months, though a January race almost guarantees some serious training weeks between Christmas and New Year. And depending on where you live, you could get some "challenging" weather on race day—freezing and rain, freezing and snow, freezing and wind.

That's gets it back to March—chow, cha, chow, chow, chow. It's still cold, especially in the mornings, though not ridiculously so. The January and February calendar is likely to be light on local races, so there will be little temptation to deviate from your training program. You can start training in the fall when the weather turns nice for running, but you can ease off during the holidays, then pick up again after New Year's. Then all you need is a killer February and you're ready to turn that mother out in March.

Running Etiquette

Running is a solitary act, but racing—especially marathons—usually involves many, many other people. Those other runners might include your training partners, your spouse, your competition, That Runner. When you go to a race, we want you to comport yourself as a model citizen of the running world. To that end, here are some suggestions to help you in that endeavor:

- Run the marathon, finish, then go back out on the course to "run people in." There is nothing that struggling runners enjoy more than seeing you come from the opposite direction. They like it so much that I would encourage you to run straight at them so they can get a good look at you. Trust me, they won't mind having to weave around you.

- Offer to pace someone in a race. If they refuse, wait on the race route and surprise them in the last miles of the race. Imagine how happy they will be to see you at Mile 18. They may not show it, but they really will want to have a conversation with you. So keep asking them questions as you run alongside them. If you run out of questions, just tell them stories about your fast marathons, especially if your times are faster than theirs.

- Together forever—or until the last tenth of a mile. Men, we really encourage you to employ this one if you run a race with your wife. Let her pace you for 26.1 miles. She may not admit it because she loves you so much, but she does not want you to draft off her for the entire race. Of course, it may not be drafting. It may be you hanging on for dear life. And then, when the finish line is in sight, sprint ahead and beat her. Perhaps try distracting her by saying: "I'm going to run ahead to take your picture." She may not immediately realize that you don't have a camera. Make sure you judge the distance correctly, lest she discover the subterfuge in time to catch and pass you.

- "You're almost there." Marathoners love irony. So if you are a spectator at a race, go stand near Mile 16 and tell the runners, "You're almost there!" or "Just around the corner!" Sure, they may shout obscenities at you or make vulgar hand gestures, but they're just being ironic, too. What they're thinking is: *That spectator is really clever. I appreciate his original use of irony at this critical juncture in the race. I believe his comment will be a critical factor in my success today.*

- If you happen to be the first in your crew to finish a race, you should wait for your friends right at the finish line. As soon as they cross, you should offer them this congratulatory salute: "What was your time?" They may be too winded to respond, but don't let up. Keep asking them until they tell you. Tell them your time and express your running bond by reminding them that they were "only" x minutes slower than you. There is no better way to forge long-lasting running relationships.

- The Offensive Line. This one requires several partners. Suppose you and three or more of your friends are more of walkers than runners. Well, there's nothing wrong with that. You should be proud of your accomplishment regardless of pace. In fact, you and your friends should be so proud that you lock arms at the beginning of the race and walk side-by-side for the first mile. Don't worry about the runners behind you. They will be so proud of you that they will be happy to go around. What's a little bottleneck in Mile 1 among friends? There are bonus points if you line up with the 7:00/mile pace group and then unfurl your Great Wall of Walkers.

/ / /

Terms, Tips, and Thoughts on Running and Running Style

Alternative Training Plans

If you hang around the sports section of your local running store, you will notice books offering "radical" and "new" and "scientific" and "ground-breaking" ways to improve your running. They include barefoot running, Chi running, running only three days per week, running on one leg, running based on the phases of the moon, and many others. Your internal governor has a name for these—gimmicks—and a message: Don't even think about it.

You have to wonder about the thinking behind these programs. With barefoot running, get this, you run barefoot. Really?! One of the best reasons to start running is to spend all your money on fancy running shoes, and then to wear those shoes at your workouts, office, and church. This program wants to deny you that shiny, cushioned joy. It makes no sense at all.

We confess that we don't understand the Chi running program, which has something to do with your stride. But we remember its predecessor, the Sigma Chi running program, where you started as a pledge, ran in Duckhead chinos and a Polo shirt, and finished your workouts with a keg stand. That program never produced any Olympic athletes to our knowledge and was eventually discontinued. We expect a similar result for this Chi program.

Another program, the three times per week plan, promises that you will run faster by running less. It sounds too good to be true, and it is. When you read the plan, you discover that every workout is vomit-inducing nightmare. So on the days when you're not running, you are curled up under your sheets dreading the next workout. Do you know how many relaxed, easy, conversational runs they prescribe in their eighteen-week workout? Zero. This program may or may not make you faster, but it will definitely have you hating running in no time.

Altitude

Runners who live and train at altitude are faster than runners who live and train at sea level. How can you hope to compete for that age-group third place in the local 5K if you're not living at least seven thousand feet above sea level? For that reason, we encourage runners to talk their spouse, under false pretenses, into letting them buy a tent. One method is to repeat for several nights how great it would be to take your son camping. Then, one night, simply ask if you can buy a tent. If she says yes, immediately go buy a Hypoxic Tent System to set up in the bedroom. Now you may not be able to train at altitude, but you'll be able to sleep at simulated altitude. And you can always roast marshmallows with your son over the stove.

Bib Number

A bib is a piece of cloth or plastic that covers the chest and is often tied around a child's neck to collect spit, drool, vomit, and an assortment of objects exiting—voluntarily or otherwise—the child's mouth. A bib number is basically the same thing and more often than not serves the same purpose. Only it has numbers on the front instead of an illustrated chick.

Boston Marathon

Boston was the site of the famous "Boston Massacre" in 1770, where British soldiers fired their muskets into a rioting crowd, killing five colonists. It is recreated every year on Patriots' Day, with the five colonists played by twenty-five thousand marathon runners and the muskets replaced by the Newton Hills. Being a part of this massacre, we mean marathon, can become an obsession worthy of Ahab or Javert, as this letter will attest:

Dear Secret Book of Running:

The B word insinuates itself in the most unlikely places, even one of those "Is it chicken or is it pork?" lunches that are the bane of the cap-toe set. To wit, I was pondering the aforesaid "chicken or pork" conundrum laid before me on institutional china when I inquired of the AARP-eligible gentleman next to me if he knew a running friend who worked at his company. He did and the following conversation ensued:

Him: Run any marathons?

Me: I'm a recovering marathoner. I limit myself to one per year.

Him: I've run fifty myself. Ever run Boston?

Me: No. I'm just over four minutes shy of qualifying.

Him: I ran six. That was back before they had these different times to qualify.

[I can hear Dana Carvey saying:"And we liked it!"]

If it was any consolation, as I cried over my plate, the tears provided just the lubrication necessary to dislodge a brick-hard square of polenta. I stopped sobbing long enough to salute this guy who laid down some blazing times during the first running boom. Six the hard way. I believe the old qualifying standard was three hours or less. And in cotton tube socks and a moustache if I had to guess. I've always followed the Groucho Marx motto that I would never want to join any club that would have me as a member. But I'll make an exception for Boston.

Car Stickers

At *The Secret Book of Running*, we do not endorse running bumper stickers. These are the white egg-on-its-side stickers with the mileage in black. The 13.1 or 26.2 stickers were bad enough, but once the triathletes got involved with the gaudy 70.3 and the even more obscene 140.6, the fad became insufferable. The boastful bumper badges are like "My Child is an Honor Roll Student" for people without children, the numerical equivalent of "I am an Honor Roll Student." [Editor's Note: *The Secret Book of Running*'s strong stand against Car Stickers has nothing to do with the market's tepid response to its 3.14 Piathlon line of stickers and apparel.]

Certified Courses and Course Certification

A certified course is a racecourse the distance of which has been certified for accuracy, typically by the United States Association for Track and Field. The process of certification involves measurements taken by an experienced measurer. The measurer must have a PhD in course measurement and at least ten years of apprenticeship in course measurement.

He (or she, of course) may spend three years measuring the cul-de-sac in front of his house before getting a crack at the local 5K. He uses a range of sophisticated tools, including wheels, surveying equipment, and unmanned drones, to take his measurements and map the course. The measurer's work then has to be approved by an official Course Certifier, whose decision is then reviewed by a seven-person panel of Supreme Certifiers. Only if the course survives all these hurdles does it become certified. Of course, if you were not satisfied with your time at the race, there is no doubt that they all got it wrong. The only logical explanation for a slow race is that the course was long. And that is so even if you ran fast last year but much slower this year on the exact same course. Just imagine how much larger last year's PR should have been had those hack certifiers did their job correctly.

Cross-training

Cross-training is like cross-dressing: Most people want to do it deep down inside, but they can never find the right time or the right shoes for it. Go ahead and cycle or swim or Zumba if you must, just do not make your internal governor jealous.

Cruise Pace

Cruise pace is that pace where the runner sets a course for adventure, his mind on a new romance.

Economy, or Running Economy

Trainers refer to running economy as the amount of energy required to achieve a desired speed. But we know that one's personal running economy is the amount of discretionary cash needed to achieve a desired finisher's medal. You may have heard that to be a runner, all you need is a pair of shoes. Not true. You try leaving your house with just a pair of shoes and you will get blisters. And arrested. You will also have to register with every county you race in, and you may notice signs posted around town with your picture on them. Those are not advertisements for RaceFoto. But without delving into criminal history, the point is that, as a runner, when you reach for your wallet, you will need a hefty credit limit on your credit card. Here, in no particular order, is the minimum amount of gear you need to race well: Racing shoes. Hip, post-race sandals. Track suit—preferably vintage Puma or Adidas. Shorts. Singlet. Gloves and arm warmers, depending on the season. Socks. Cap or visor or beanie, depending on the season. Watch with heart-rate monitor and GPS functionality. Sunglasses. Custom-made chip holder. It goes without saying that all of this gear should be constructed using the latest in moisture-wicking, sweat-converting-to-a-combination-of-cologne (or perfume)-and-magical-energy-juice-that-seeps-back-into-your-body technology. It must also be name brand and part of a collection shown within the last year in Paris, Milan, or New York Fashion Week. You are guaranteed an age-group award if you wear something that Anna Wintour was photographed in while on a treadmill.

Won't all this be expensive? Yes, prohibitively so. And we haven't even talked about the application fees, the travel costs (fir goodness sake, don't cramp your legs in coach), the hotel rooms (the higher the star rating, the greater the PR), the post-race spa treatments (massages, clay wraps,

Ayurvedic therapy, Aura Soma readings), and the mortgage-busting meals that accompany every race (and we recommend a minimum of ten races per year, each in a different major American city or "destination") But without your purchases, the running economy will grind to a halt. You have to do your part to stimulate the economy. Besides, why let a little thing like lack of credit get in the way of your goals and dreams? The back of those debt collection letters are great for calculating your monthly mileage. Is it possible to race well without buying all this gear? Absolutely not. You know, those elite runners get all their cool stuff for free. Don't you resent them even more, now? Let that resentment fuel your training so you can beat them. And if you can't beat them, join them. Or mug them to pay for your gear.

Explanations

It is seldom advisable to tell all, especially when all represents a multitude of planetary thoughts, feelings, and conditions orbiting around you during the marathon. Be sparing, for instance, with phrases like "I would have" or "I could have." Let the time speak for itself. Race reports heavily weighted with qualifiers like "if" or "if only" or "had it not been" are annoying, especially when the qualifier suggests a Herculean effort on the part of the marathoner. "If the last tribesmen of the Chippewa Nation had not materialized at Mile 16 and shot flaming arrows into my calf, hamstring, and buttock, I know I would have run a negative split." Inexperienced runners do this, apparently, in the belief that they need to provide context for other runners, the context being that the time is not representative of their true fitness level. But runners who finished ahead of you don't care about your time, and won't until it challenges their own. And runners who finished behind you would prefer not to hear you tell them not only that you were faster than them, but how much faster than them you could have been. The more civilized approach is to discuss your time when you have the rapt attention of an audience who cares, such as in an elevator or bank teller line.

Gyms

Runners often ask us: Should I get a gym membership? If you can afford it, yes, because it offers you climate-controlled sanctuary from the elements, treadmill access, and—depending on the gym—a variety of cross-training options. You could take Pilates or yoga (or as they call it at my gym: "Rate My Thong"). When I'm finished running at the gym, we like to do our patented five-minute free-weight circuit. This is where we can do a complete "beach" workout of chest, lats, biceps, and triceps in five minutes or less, depending on how long we stay pinned underneath the bench-press bar.

Lactate Threshold

This is the exercise intensity at which lactic acid starts to accumulate in the blood faster than it can be metabolized, or removed, by the body. Think of Lucille Ball in front of the conveyor belt at the point when she can't put any more chocolates in her mouth. That's lactate threshold. Lactate threshold has nothing to do with breast-feeding or breast-feeding runners, at least not in the way you're thinking.

Negative Split

The negative split is the process by which a runner completes the second half of a race slightly faster than the first half. Many coaches and elite athletes believe that running a negative split is the key to optimal race performance. Many casual runners, especially marathoners, believe the negative split is like the Loch Ness Monster or Bigfoot. It can't be proven, has rarely been seen, and exists primarily in myth.

Pace Bands

Pace bands are paper or plastic bracelets you see adorning the wrists of marathon runners. From a distance, it looks like they were all just released from the hospital. The bracelet lists the split times to run a predetermined finishing time for the marathon. These are best avoided, because it is a known fact that runners are constitutionally unable to wear a pace band unless it shows a finishing time at least ten minutes faster than the capabilities of the runner. The runner knows this, but like pirated cable, she simply can't resist. The bands have a tiny microchip inside, and at about Mile 10, they begin to broadcast this message: "I told you so!" or "This is not a typo. You're just slow." Pace bands use a powerful bonding adhesive, so the runner's attempt to chew the damn thing off during the race is always in vain. But at least it can be cut off back at the hotel. Runners are strenuously urged, in no uncertain terms, to avoid the Pace Tattoo, despite its novelty. Otherwise, their marathon implosion will come with a scarlet letter (numbers?) for all to see at the post-race party, and they will find themselves scrubbing their forearm like Karen Silkwood and urging, "Out, out, damn splits!"

PR Envy

Sigmund Freud, a popular middle-distance runner in fin-de-siècle Vienna, popularized this theory of psychoanalysis, which refers to the anxiety felt by a runner over his training partner's race times. Often referred to colloquially as "mine is *smaller* than yours" syndrome, PR Envy can be a debilitating condition most acutely felt during post-race activities where the runner sulks and eats too many donuts while waiting for his training partner (whom he drove to the race) to collect his age-group award. The condition has increased in the last decade, as advances in race time and Internet fact checking have made lying about PR size more difficult. The condition may leech into training strategies and group runs, where the sufferer of PR envy will attempt to "out race" his partner in the last half mile of the workout. In many cases, the sufferer will attempt to overcome the condition by running the first half of his races well faster than his skill level only to fade drastically down the stretch, resulting in a significantly slower finishing time. The moment when the runner realizes that his splits are getting longer, that he went out too fast, and that his partner will beat him yet again is known as crashtration anxiety.

Port-O-Let Squatter

If you find yourself at a major racing event, the kind with tens of thousands of runners, and you have to get to the start area hours before the race will begin, do not hesitate to squat in a port-o-let. And we don't mean squat in the "evacuation complete" sense. Here we use the word to mean "to take up temporary residence in property you do not own." This is an especially useful tactic if it is a particularly cold or wet morning. We like to pack a Pine Tree air freshener for these situations (and a bandana in case the stench kills the Pine Tree faster than the Dung Beetle.) We will wait (or cut) in line, enter the port-o-let, and then stay there until ten minutes before race time. You can sit down, listen to your iPod, do some standing stretches and deep knee bends, all while avoiding the outside elements. It is entirely possible for you to have a breakfast picnic in there, though legal counsel has advised that we cannot explicitly recommend that to you. We can say that if you sit at the right angle, you can nap at least as comfortably as on an airplane (and that includes first-class). Think of the energy you can conserve. Pity those runners shivering outside or getting soaked in the rain. If anyone bangs on the door, just say: "Almost finished!" or "Sorry! Clams!" or "Possession is nine-tenths of the law!" They should move on to one of the other available port-o-lets and leave you alone. But if it sounds like they're forming a posse to flip you over, be prepared to make a hasty exit. Keep your head down as you leave and don't forget your air freshener.

Race Results Rave

Is there a more wonderful sport than running? A race begins and ends with a communal gathering of participants. Before the race, when hope springs eternal, runners crowd tightly into corrals behind the starting line. Everyone is happy and friendly and you could crush another runner's foot and the only response would be: "No worries!" When the gun goes off, everyone is considerate and the crowd looks out for every runner. Trampling is out of the question. After the race, there is a markedly different gathering. It occurs around the race results—several sheets of 8½ x 11" paper with columns of results that always seem to be in eight-point font. Somebody shouts: "The results are up!" and a great cluster of a scrum forms around those telling sheets as if Moses had brought them down from Mount Sinai. The mood is decidedly testier than it was just a short time ago in the corral, for the pre-race euphoria has yielded to post-race reality. Runners crowd around, elbowing each other, jostling and pushing, avoiding eye contact, and why? Because they think those tiny columns in Helvetica bold might somehow offer a time different and better than what is on their watch and in their recent memory. In this communal gathering, one often hears such pleasantries as "What? No breakdown by age group?" and "Find your time and move on, jerk wad!"

"Runner's Race"

If you hear someone refer to an upcoming race as a "runner's race," it's best to avoid it. That runner, for whom this race purportedly "is," is no one you want to be associated with. First, she's probably naturally fast. She's definitely not wearing basketball culottes and the race T-shirt at the start line. Second, she doesn't consider it her birthright to have a technical fabric T-shirt and a finisher's medal for her twenty-dollar registration fee. Third, she is indifferent to whether the course is certified or merely guesstimated. Finally, she eschews timing chips. And you, my friend, do not eschew timing chips. You do that which is the exact opposite of eschew—chew?—when it comes to timing chips. You put all this in the blender and you get an unpleasant morning with nothing to show for it and no chance of coming home with age-group treasure.

Runner Vision

The schedule says one thing, the runner sees another. It is a common malady. It seems to inflict most runners, ironically, when they are injured or fatigued or going through a sub-par pace. Their schedule may say five easy miles plus strides, but because of the Runner Vision, the runner will see 8 x 1-mile at your fastest mile time ever with fifteen-step recovery, you miserable excuse for a marathoner.

Schwag

Schwag refers to the promotional items and trinkets that that you receive in exchange for your race registration fee. You should run, or at least enter, each race with a sense of entitlement. That means your schwag should, at a minimum, include a race T-shirt. And we don't mean a cotton or 50/50 blend T-shirt. No, it has to be a technical or performance shirt, something that sounds like NASA created it. Avoid any race that requires you to finish it to receive your shirt. Imagine the effrontery of that race director to even suggest such a thing. You will also want a medal, a real Olympic-weight one. A pair of socks would be nice, too. Chapstick and a mini Body Glide is always a nice addition to a schwag bag. We also expect a bottle of Chanel No. 5, two round-trip tickets on Virgin Airways, and a $150 Starbucks Card. The schwag bag itself should be of a reusable material so can use it for groceries. None of this is too much to ask for your twenty-dollar entry fee and your lending your name and prestige to the race. It is for the same reason that you should demand a climate-controlled starting corral with turndown service.

Split. Splits

A split is the time it takes to cover a particular fixed distance in a race or workout. In American road racing, splits are usually measured in miles. On the track, meters are the preferred unit of measurement. In Arthur Dazs's ground-breaking work with middle distance runners in the 1950s, first published in the *Annals of Performance* under the title "The Effect of B-Split Consumption on A-Split Performance: A Randomized Trial," Dazs showed that runners who incorporated nightly banana splits into their training diet ran slower splits than those who ate bananas without the other split accouterments. The prevailing theory at the time, based on a slender treatise published by a group of Wisconsin researchers under the title "Lickety-Split Results," held that copious consumption of banana splits improved split times at all distances. This split in the literature led to vigorous debate in the running academy, with Dazs's findings ultimately prevailing after it was discovered that the Wisconsin researchers had secretly accepted funding from the dairy industry.

Spouses at the Start Line

A common practice in marathoning, particularly among runners new to the marathon, is to bring their spouse to the start line. Sometimes there is a small child in tow. This seems to be a particular problem for the male runner who, oblivious to the weather conditions, honestly believes that his wife (and the little tyke just getting over the flu) wants to watch him stand in a starting corral at six a.m. in the morning. He will typically reward her generous spirit with these words of thanks: "Here, hold my stuff." This condition is usually cured when the wife takes up marathoning herself and quickly becomes a better runner. At that point, she reciprocates his words of thanks with this heartfelt valentine: "I'll wait for you at the finish line."

Step-ahead Syndrome

Step-ahead Syndrome is a condition that affects runners, usually your training partner. It manifests itself in an inability of the runner to run alongside other runners. Rather, he or she must always run at least one step ahead. You can either resent or pity the runner. Consider this true-life story and make your decision.

Dear Secret Book of Running:

I did not cry when they loaded my running partner into the back of the ambulance. I did not wail and have to be restrained like Sean Penn in Mystic River. I showed no anger, I betrayed no emotion. But when you run with the same person for four or five months, you tend to develop a bond, a connection, an umbilical relationship. Losing your partner can be like losing a limb. Well, maybe not a whole limb, maybe just some skin off the limb or perhaps a long toenail. Anyway, when you look down at your partner immobilized on a stretcher, and when the paramedics wrap a neck brace around him and feed him into the backside of an ambulance, it is only natural that your emotions would get the fast-pass to Space Mountain. But as I said, I didn't cry. I was stoic like the Sphinx. Not Leon Sphinx the boxer, the Sphinx outside that hotel in Las Vegas. On that fateful morning, I did not let the paramedics or bystanders see my true feelings. But if emotions were dishwashing liquid, mine would have been Joy—extra-strength and lemon fresh Joy. Had the paramedics brought me into the hospital and took my X-ray, the radiologist would have held up the film, pointed four times, and surmised: "This would indicate that he has joy, joy, joy, joy down in his heart." And if a confused young intern asked, "Where?" the radiologist would have patiently answered, "Down in his heart."

But let's return to my running partner, for it was he, not I, speeding to the emergency room. At the hospital, the doctors confirmed what I secretly suspected: broken neck. Ow, you might say. How, you might ask? Well therein lies the tale. Your typical broken neck results from a traumatic episode like a car crash, snap mare off the top turnbuckle, or mixing alcohol and trampolines. But the doctors determined, again as I suspected, that his break was an overuse injury. The doctors explained that his neck was like a suicidal fast-food cashier working during the peak summer months. After weeks and weeks of steady pressure, it finally snapped.

Could my running partner have avoided this cruel fate? I don't want to make any snap judgments, but probably not. My running partner was born with a genetic condition called SAS— Step-ahead Syndrome. I noticed the symptoms on our first run together. About five steps down the road, my partner start running faster than me—exactly one step faster. If I sped up, he sped up, too—one step's worth. If I slowed down, he slowed, too, until he was, yes, one step ahead. I did not think much of it on that first day. Giving him the benefit of the doubt, I thought perhaps he was just being polite and allowing me to draft.

Four months later, I began to understand the chronic nature of his condition. Another day, another run, and another step ahead. He could have had a naked picture of my mama airbrushed on the front of his shirt. I would have never known because, despite the wide distribution of those shirts on eBay, I never saw my partner's front side. He was always one step ahead. It could be raining or it could be 95 degrees. I could be flying or I could be shuffling. It simply didn't matter. He was right there with me, the consummate runner: indefatigable, inspirational, and in front by a step. You hear people say, "He's the type of guy you'd want in a foxhole with you." Well, my running partner was the type of person you'd want when you had to leave the foxhole, go through the booby-trapped jungle, and traverse a land-mine field.

You might think that those runs would get boring, but you'd be more wrong than a breeder of Golden doodles. You see, my running partner was very conversational and engaging. It's just that he was a victim of his genes and couldn't overcome the Step-ahead Syndrome. And that is what led to his broken neck. He ran all our training runs with his neck craned about 75 degrees so he could look back and talk to me. Depending on my position, it was like running with a coin for a partner. It had to be painful for him. Half the time he would run off the curb or into traffic because he was too busy looking backwards at me. It got so bad that I recommended he get one of those mirror gadgets that cyclists wear. You know the thing I'm talking about—it looks like someone speared them in the side of the head with a dental instrument.

Did it get annoying? Well, he did have this congenital genetic defect. But that begs the question. Yes, yes it was annoying. Day after day, always in the lead, the constant looking back, it's enough to make one think dark thoughts, thoughts such as—well, let's just say that in craning his neck to keep an eye on me, he was doing his own part to reduce the local criminal docket by one. The selfless-ness of this guy! We were in the last week of our taper, and owl-boy was in front of me as usual, and I was daydreaming about running along a high mountain pass—a pass with no shoulder and sharp, jagged rocks below—and Sir Twist-A-Lot was asking questions like, "So, how you doing back there?" when we heard the snap.

I didn't expect my partner to run again, but he had one of those miraculous recoveries reserved for movies of the week during sweeps season. By some miracle of medicine, the doctors gave him some neck transplant and he made it to the starting line of our marathon. He was completely focused, staring directly forward as we waited for the start. It may have been his game face or it may have been the newly fused metal plates just below his ears. Whatever it was, he was almost back to normal. And wouldn't you know it, he ran that entire race the same way he ran our training runs—one step ahead of me. I'll never understand how he did it. No matter, at least he didn't turn back to talk to me. Not once. Doctor's orders, I would come to learn. What's more, my finisher's medal looked so much better on me. Draped around my neck, I looked like an Olympian. My partner wanted the same look, I know it, but the volunteers couldn't get it over his metal halo. My heart went out to him. Well, it almost did. It stopped one step short.

Taper. Tapering

This is the final phase in a training cycle, occurring anywhere from a couple of days to a couple of weeks before the target race. In theory, it is a time to reduce training quantity, sharpen essential race attributes, and minimize overall stress. In practice, it is a time when the runner forgets the previous eighteen weeks of training and convinces herself that the target race is no different from a final exam, and, for that reason, must be prepared for like a final exam—by cramming. It is also a time when a chemical reaction in the brain causes the runner to ignore all nonessential race distractions (work, family, paying the electricity bill) so that the runner may obsess about the target race for nineteen hours per day. The final phase of the taper, which often occurs on race morning in the race chute, is called the "good faith estimate." This is when the runner, despite all evidence to the contrary, decides that she can run the marathon fifteen minutes faster than her training would indicate.

Trail Running and Trail Races

Trail running is for runners who want to run on "gorgeous, scenic trails through some of the most beautiful wilderness in the area," and then spend the entire run staring down at their feet so they don't trip over a root or rock. Those that take a chance on looking around to take in the scenery quickly become Frank Sinatra runners—they pick themselves up and get back in the race. No, the only benefit to racing on trails is that no one knows what is or isn't a fast time at these races. That and the off chance that your competition may get lost in the woods.

Ultra Running

Ultra runners are the Taliban-like offshoot of marathoners. These are men and women who want to run more than the marathon distance (in one day), want to do it in the woods on billy-goat grade hills, if possible, and would like to eat a pizza while doing so. In one of those great chicken-and-egg conundrums, it is not know whether ultra running causes men to grow beards and pony-tails or whether the beards and pony-tails cause men to become ultra-runners.

VO2Max

VO2Max is a measure of the maximum oxygen consumption or aerobic capacity of a runner. It is distinguished from V82Max, which is the maximum amount of tomato juice that a runner can consume at a single sitting.

///

Conclusion

If you have made it this far, then you now know all the secrets of running. You are armed with all the knowledge you will ever need to run faster than ever. That Runner (they know who they are and so do we) may not know it, but his or her racing and training dominance will soon be over. So we wish you happy running in the future. May your heart be filled with joy and serenity, may your aura glow, may you be at peace and one with all mankind and nature, may the birds and little creatures of the forest chirp for you the way they did for Snow White. And may you use this spirit of peace and harmony to go out and humiliate your racing opponents. And should we cross paths in the starting corral—we'll be the ones in the short shorts—remember where you learned your secrets and go easy on a slow and humble runner.

Thank You Sponsors
The Secret Book of Running staff would like to acknowledge the following sponsors, without whom this book would not have been possible. Please consider purchasing their products if you have money left over after buying a dozen copies of our book.

AIR CHERUIYOT. Inspired by a pair worn by Robert Cheruiyot when he won the Chicago Marathon in 2006, the Air Cheruiyot is a super-light racing flat with just the right amount of stability and durability. The mesh upper and reinforced sock liner keep your foot snug and comfortable, while the side and rear airbags provide peace-of-mind and safety should the race directors lay out a Slip-and-Slide at the finish line of your next marathon. Men's Sizes 8–14. Banana-peel Yellow or Black Ice. $169.99.

CHEATAH COACHING SYSTEMS. Want to qualify for Boston but you think you're too slow, and besides, you don't want to train? Well, sulk no more. Cheatah Coaching and its stable of ex–cross country stars desperately in need of cash will get you to Hopkinton in no time. Here's how it works: You register for a Boston-qualifying marathon and then meet with one of our "coaches" after you visit the expo. We'll take your chip and number and run the race for you. That's right—no long runs, no mile repeats, no sweat. Sign up with us, and you'll be running like a Cheatah in no time. [Note to Parents: Is this a gift for your high school son or daughter? Consider bundling this gift with Cheatah's "Beat the SAT" Program.] $750 plus airfare and hotel accommodations (3-star or better) to target marathon.

2010 BEST OF THE TRAINING LOGS. This book, which the *New York Review* called a "riveting read" and *Runner's World* praised as "a work of profound literary merit," painstakingly collects training logs from runners of all skill levels across the country. The book will enthrall the runner on your holiday list with passages like "5 miles about 42 min cold outside" and "15 minutes is plantar back?" Incarcerated runner Rick Monroe raves: "I read that sucka like five times in a row." Hardcover, 624 pages. $29.95.

GELOTTA HOME GEL-MAKING KIT. Do you find yourself always heading to the local running store to stock up on Gu and Powergel? Are you dissatisfied with the limited flavors available? Then you need the Gelotta Home Gel-Making Kit. With this kit, you can make your own energy gels from the comfort of your own home. And you won't be stuck with strawberry-banana any longer. All you need are leftovers. The Gelotta does all the work with its patented "set it and forget it" technology, slurping out fresh gel into edible sausage casing in about fifteen minutes. In no time, you'll be refueling to sweetbreads, foie gras, or red beans and rice home gels. A happier stomach means better performances. Three-month supply of casing included. $139.95.

HUMMER ARMOUR TRAINING GEAR. Tired of being chased off the road by careless drivers? Scared you might get run over by some do-gooder in a late-model Prius because he's too busy tuning into NPR to pay attention to the road? You're not alone. And that's why the makers of Hummer trucks and Under Armour apparel collaborated on the Hummer Armour line of training gear. Made of welded steel and polished chrome, you can run with confidence when you wear these tights and tops. It's payback time, Prius boy. We Must Protect This House Like Nothing Else. Running lights sold separately. Dry clean only. Tights, $89.95. Tops, $79.95.

GARMIN 501 FORERUNNER "SUDOKU" VERSION. The latest offering from Garmin has all the features you expect from its high-tech line of personal trainers—time, pace, distance, heart rate, lottery numbers, course difficulty expressed as a *Wine Spectator* ranking. But what makes this model different is that it does not automatically display the information for you. Instead, it scrambles all the numbers into a challenging, multi-level Sudoku puzzle. Solve the first puzzle and it displays your time. Solve the next and you get your distance. And so on, and so forth. The Garmin 501—Because Running Is Mental. Comes with stylus and scratch pad. $379.99.

FUEL BELT "FINISHER" HYDRATION BELT. Fuel Belt had the marathoner who "just hopes to finish" in mind when it designed the Finisher. The engineers at Fuel Belt realized that this runner may start in the morning but may not finish until late afternoon. And who wants to drink Gatorade all that time? Yuck. The Finisher includes a mini coffee/espresso maker on one side (the optional steam pipe will froth milk and scorch other runners who get too close), a "Do The Dew" fountain drink dispenser on the other, and, to reward yourself when you pass twenty miles, a soft-serve machine. Total Capacity: 8 venti coffee drinks, 4 liters of soda, 2 gallons of ice cream. $695. Many runners who purchased the Finisher also purchased the Fuel Belt Micro-Microwave Pack with six months' supply of Hot Pockets.

///

About the Author

Lance P. Martin is a middle-aged, middle-of-the-pack runner who never ran track or cross-country. He is a veteran of over a dozen marathons, a former member of and coach for a chapter of the Leukemia and Lymphoma Society's Team in Training Program, a Boston Marathon qualifier and finisher, and a blogger on the tension between the love of marathon running and the love of good food and wine. He lives in Asheville, North Carolina with his wife, Anne Conquest, and their two sons, Max and Leo.

His email address is lancepmartin@gmail.com.

Made in the USA
Lexington, KY
29 September 2011